A YEAR OF Thanksgivings

A MEMOIR

SALLIE READ HICKS

with Joseph N. Davis

Talking Tree Tales

First Edition: 2018

Hardback ISBN 9780692976210

Ebook ISBN 9780692976227

Talking Tree Tales

Making History One Life at a Time

TalkingTreeTales.wordpress.com

talkingtreetales@gmail.com

Nashville, Tennessee 37221

A CHILD'S BLESSING

Thank you for the world so sweet.

Thank you for the things we eat.

Thank you for the birds that sing.

Thank you, God, for everything.

~Edith Rutter Leatham

TABLE OF CONTENTS

CHAPTER IV: COURTSHIP

CHAPTER V: OUR WEDDINGS DAY

CHAPTER VI: CHRISTMAS RECOLLECTIONS

CHAPTER VII: A ROSE FOR COURAGE

CHAPTER VIII: THE COLOR OF NAMES

CHAPTER IX: A LIFE OF FAITH

CHAPTER X: FAMILY LIFE

CHAPTER XII: LOOKING AHEAD

EPILOGUE

AFTERWORD

CHRONOLOGY, GENEALOGY, & FAMILY PHOTOGRAPHS

INTRODUCTION

Anyone who makes his or her way through these pages will come to understand why it is that my sisters and I wanted so much for my mother to record her memories—she is something special. That was certainly true of her own mother as well, and although it always seemed incongruous to me that a second sequential only-child would have had six children, as her fourth child, I am more than grateful that she did. Families collide in marriage and unpredictable adventures ensue; readers of this book will also come to an appreciation of the uniqueness of my father's indomitable character. Pondering how two people so different from one another could have formed such a totally committed bond as they enjoyed is one of the joys of reading here about their lives.

Unfortunately, my mother has had to contend all her life with shortcomings of her eyesight as a result of congenital cataracts that came to her family entirely out of the blue and also afflicted two of her children but have now completely disappeared without a trace from any of her twelve grandchildren. For most it would have been a greater burden, but for her it was a minor cross to bear that she accepted and completely transcended.

Throughout my adult life, friends and acquaintances of my mother have made special efforts to tell me how much they love her. Naturally, this includes her friends, but also shopkeepers and service providers who say things like "We all just love it when Sallie comes in—she's our favorite customer. She is so special." Of course, I know she is, but I've always marveled at the fact that people who barely know her "get it." How does she do it? It actually gives me faith in the current state of humanity that so many recognize and respond to a genuinely exceptional psychology like hers.

But it's one thing to appreciate grace like hers and another thing altogether to incarnate it. Who is going to keep her spirit alive? My five sisters are each thoroughly lovable, but we would all admit that none of us measure up to her almost supernatural endowment of thoughtfulness and sensitivity. I imagine how much less enchanted our lives would be had Marcel Proust not shared his remembrances of a fascinating world that is now long gone, and I worry that when my mother goes, she will take all of her fascinating world with her.

So when I saw in a recent high-school alumni magazine that my childhood friend Joe Davis was offering to help people pen their memoirs, and after a month or so of my usual cluelessness, I belatedly realized that it might not be too late. Joe has an English degree and is a former teacher, as well as an Episcopal priest; and I finally appreciated the fact that, with his patient and benevolent collaboration, my mother might be able to tell elements of her story in a way that would reach through mere details to convey at least some of the essence of how she responded to all the unexpected things, both good and bad, that she encountered over the course of her years. And so we initiated a humble process that took off beyond what I could have imagined. Joe would come over on Mondays from the late fall of 2015 through the spring of 2016, and my mother would recount some of her favorite memories, and from those meetings Joe put together this book that might have been called *Mondays with Joe*. It became a fitting testament to more than a few great lives well lived, as well as a wonderful keepsake of her own unique and beautiful spirit.

There is perhaps one other incident that led to the creation of this book. I was fortunate to have studied at Stanford University under the guidance of the renowned Mallarmé (and Proust) scholar Robert Greer Cohn, with whom I have kept up a lively correspondence over the years. In the summer of 2009, my wife and young son Thomas traveled with my mother (her last "big trip") to Monterey and to Dr. Cohn's residence in Menlo Park, where the two of them conducted a delightful meeting, each of them recounting many of their childhood experiences. Thoroughly charmed—and as I had expected, the feeling was mutual—Dr. Cohn remarked on the almost literary quality of her commentary and expressed the conviction that my mother must surely write down some of her memories before they were lost. She and I both dismissed the idea as unlikely, but his judgment was true and I am so grateful that we found a way for her to accomplish it.

George T. Hicks, II
Fourth child and only son

April 24, 2017

CHAPTER I
In The Beginning

Pewee Valley

I am intimidated by the need to start somewhere if I am to tell the story of my life. The memories don't come to me in any particular order. I could jump in the middle, almost anywhere, and work my way backwards and forwards, and I would be perfectly happy. I am told that this method would have the complete approval of Mark Twain, who recommended starting anywhere and saying whatever came to mind, following one's inspiration from story to story. Since this is the way my scattered mind works, I have little real choice but to proceed in this manner; but please don't give me credit for following a particular writer in his method. For me, it's quite an accident if my mind inclines me toward a method used by anyone who knew what he was doing.

Even so, I suppose it would be best to start with Pewee Valley. I think I was three or four when we lived in Pewee Valley, Kentucky, and I have some very early memories of it. I have other, earlier memories, of times and places that my mother said I couldn't possibly remember, except that I used to describe places and people and events to her, and she would say, "You can't remember that!" But I did.

My memories of Pewee Valley are different from those earlier ones. I remember it with great clarity, and not just in flashes. I loved it, and those years there had a bearing on the rest of my life. Pewee Valley was almost Disneyesque, and I have never seen anything like it since then. It was not a little village. It was a kind of artists' colony for literary people and musicians. It was no garden spot in the winter, but it was a real gathering spot in the summertime.

We moved there in 1932 and leased a house. Most of the winter we lived in an apartment in Louisville, but our house was way out in the country. My father sometimes made business trips to Louisville, which meant crossing the railroad tracks six times, and the weather was sometimes very bad. My mother lived in absolute terror of his coming and going because usually he went in the car, and she was afraid of his crossing the tracks that many times. Occasionally he had to go on the train. She didn't worry about his riding the train. There were many things for grown-ups to worry about, but I was too young to worry, and she was too wise to let me know that she was worried. I remember a discussion at the depot once about an accident, but it didn't occur to me to think my father was not safe.

The depot was one of several gathering places in the town. It was an old fashioned depot, a white clapboard building like every depot there along the railroad tracks. People would run into each other coming and going there. Another meeting place was the grocery store, which you had to cross the railroad tracks to reach. You either went to Mr. Foley's or Mr. Million's grocery. You didn't go to both. We were Mr. Million's customers. We would have to go up two sets of wooden steps to get into Mr. Million's grocery, which was really quite high. His prices were high, too, a little higher than Mr. Foley's, but my mother thought it was worth it to shop there. For one thing, he had excruciatingly good cookies. Somebody in the community made them and would bring them in, and they didn't stay long before people bought them. I don't have the vaguest idea what they cost, but it was well worth climbing the stairs and paying any amount to get them. Mother would bring them home every two or three weeks. When mother came home with cookies, it was a great day.

Mr. Foley was a short, very friendly man who always wore a hat and a leather apron. Although we weren't supposed to shop with both grocers, my mother bought one thing from him on the QT: black-market meat.

Anybody who went to Pewee Valley was affected by its topography. Everything was either up or down. It wasn't mountainous; it was just really hilly. When it snowed, you had a choice of all kinds of sledding.

If you went anywhere in our hilly town, you passed by the post office, over which Miss Lucy presided as postmistress, and she would notice you going by. She also was the telephone operator, so she knew everything that happened in the whole town. I wouldn't call her a "busybody," but she was a great source of information. If you needed to know anything, you knew you could ask Miss Lucy.

Our phone number was 203, just three digits, like everyone else's, and no number was used twice. That should give you an idea how many people lived in Pewee Valley. Now if I wanted to make a telephone call, I stood on the box in our back hall, which was always kind of chilly, and I'd turn the crank round and round. When it made a loud noise, I'd pick up the receiver and see if Miss Lucy was available. Usually she would answer, and if she did, she would know that I or my mother or father was on the line. She would say to me, "Sallie, are you looking for your mother?" As a rule, I was so young that

I only called Miss Lucy when I wanted to find out what was going on. But if my mother wanted to call Mrs. Johnson, for instance, Miss Lucy had to make the connection, for she was the operator that everybody had to go through to make any phone call. It was a party line. That's partly why Miss Lucy knew everything. She was also the postmistress, so she knew all the letters that went to anybody and every letter that anybody sent.

She would say, "The mail hasn't come yet," or "Your mother is gone to Mrs. Johnson's," or "There's a meeting at the church." She knew it would be St. James that I was interested in because that was the church we went to. My mother went there two or three times a week. From her perch at the post office, she could always see what coming and going there was, so I could ring the bell and ask her where my mother was. She would always tell me. She would know if my mother was at Mrs. Johnson's for a meeting having to do with the church or having to do with something about books. She knew just about everything that happened. And you didn't want to do something that you weren't supposed to do because she would know about it and tell your parents. I was too young to be able to do something I wasn't supposed to do, but she knew where everybody was. For example, she knew when the boys had gone off on their bikes and were not in class. She knew who wasn't in school. To go to school you caught a bus at the depot right in front of the post office, and she saw who got on that bus for the ride to school in Anchorage, which was the next town.

I went to the post office occasionally with my mother when she went to pick up her mail. It was not thirty feet from Mr. Foley's store. I would see Miss Lucy putting the mail in the slots. I always thought the mail was delivered by train to the depot, so it came by way of Louisville. Sometimes it would get there late, and people would be calling to find out if the mail had arrived. Miss Lucy would say, "No, don't come yet," or "I'm not done yet," or "Yes, the mail is up now."

We lived in a house that was not ours. It was down Ash Avenue, past several stone gateposts and many curves. One curve went over a little creek; then you climbed up the hill. It was a gradual climb, though it was steep in places. You would go to the top of the hill and turn left and there was the gravel driveway to our house and gate, which was always open as far as I knew.

Our house was normally rented out as a summer house, so it had no heating system. One had been jerry-rigged and put in. We had six fireplaces, and we used them on cold days. Charlie was the very nice man who laid the fires every morning. Ruth was his wife, and she had two babies, so we didn't see her very often. They lived close by. Charlie would lay the fires and then he would light them when you first got up in the morning. I didn't have one in my room. The house had a center hall that was about sixteen to twenty feet long. Double doors led into the living room, which had a fireplace. There was a large, open, covered porch. If you went the other way through the center-hall double doors, you went into the dining room. It had a fireplace which usually had a fire going in it, except in the heat of the summer. It opened onto a large screened-in porch. We ate on that porch a good bit. The kitchen was to the right, sort of in the front. You went that way to the garage, which was detached, needless to say. There was a chicken coop behind the garage. Charlie and Ruth and their two babies lived back there near the chicken coop. Ruth took care of the chickens and that sort of thing. She didn't help with the cooking very often.

Eleanora had moved to Pewee with us from Nashville to help my mother and look after me. I don't know where Eleanora lived, but I remember her very well and her daughter Catherine, who was about my age, and her little brother, who was called "Brother." Across the driveway was a large grassy area with lots of flowers in it. A double row of irises went up to the grape arbor, which produced large, succulent grapes each year. It also had a cherry tree, but you had to fight the birds off as soon as the cherries came in. If you got one good cook pot of cherries, that was about the best you could do; otherwise, it was like that movie The Birds and you were fighting off a raiding party of birds while the other birds watched from a short distance. I never saw a bird close up enough to know quite what they look like, but I have an image in my mind, and that movie always made me think about the battle of cherry tree.

The McAfee Sisters

If you kept going straight on the road that led to our house, it would take you to the cabin. That log cabin was a big piece of magic. It stood two stories tall, and it was designed so that it had a summer side and a winter side with a dogtrot in the middle. Two elderly ladies lived there. I believe the son of one of them owned the property where they lived. I knew these ladies as Miss Annie and Miss Leal. Miss Annie was small, pink, and gold, with white hair and plump little hands just like a storybook fairy godmother. She told wonderful stories. She and her sister were the McAfee sisters. Annie married Mr. Dulaney, who owned that property. I don't know Miss Leal's past, but I always got the story that she had had a very sad young womanhood. She and her sister were very close. Miss Leal always wore brown, even in the summer, thin dresses with a brown pattern all over. She was very ambulatory. Miss Annie really was not. I don't think there was a wheelchair, but I never saw her walk. I saw her in different places but I don't know what the conveyance was.

They had tea every afternoon, and when I got so I didn't spill things so much, I was invited to come and have tea with them. They called it "cambric tea." They didn't have cambric tea, but they served it to me. It was tea made with milk and sugar. It was quite English when you come to think about it. Miss Annie and Miss Leal enjoyed having a little girl come to tea, so I was treated very royally when I got there. They had china but mostly they used pewter. I know they used soap to clean the dishes and utensils, because I saw the soap in their little kitchen, but the dishes were always just a little bit oily. I wasn't too sure how clean things really were, and I must have said something to Mother about it. She said, "I don't think they have any liquid dishwashing detergent like what we use in the kitchen here, but I think the dishes are all right for you to use." They also made apricot ice cream in the summer with a crank. It never got quite frozen. They would serve it in a porringer with a handle on it, a child's porringer, and a spoon that was a little oily, but you could overlook that.

You had to go through the screened-in dogtrot to enter the cabin. I didn't know how old the house was, but I didn't care. I just knew it was old. They would always latch the door. But Miss Leal would always come and let you in. Anybody could have walked right in without any trouble anyway, but she would always come to the door and invite you in. You went to the right, to the living room, and it had a fireplace. Charlie went up there to lay that fire, too. It was a big, dark room, but it felt warm, and in the winter it was wonderful. There was a little door that went out and down the hall to the right to a small bedroom, the winter bedroom, where Miss Annie's bed was. Her room was always full of sunshine. Miss Leal's bed was in the summer end of the house. It was a pretty little canopy bed up from the dogtrot. Hollyhocks grew outside her window. They were taller than I was. There were maybe six or eight in a row right up against the house. I thought anything so pink would have to be wonderful. I remember going to see if they had a nice fragrance. Instead, they had a bee! Hollyhocks always seem to have bees. I took a deep breath, and I got a bee sting right in the middle of my forehead. Miss Annie and Miss Leal were so solicitous. They got a little ice out, wrapped it in a linen cloth, and held it up to my forehead. They made me hold it there until I went home. It wasn't an ordeal, but I was offended. I had just wanted to smell a flower! I thought you could trust a flower. I learned not to smell hollyhocks.

Pewee Valley was very green all the time, except in the wintertime, when it was covered in deep snow. There were no children around to play with except for when Mr. Woodford's sons, Miss Annie's grandchildren, came and we played. There were steps leading up from the dogtrot to the second floor of the cabin. In the peak of the roof above Ms. Annie's bedroom was a room we were allowed to go to. There we made up plays and acted them out. The boys were a little older than I, and they were very patient with this little girl. We played whatever we thought was good theater. We all listened to an early morning radio program on Saturdays called *Let's Pretend.* I was allowed to get up as early as I wanted on Saturday and listen to it on my radio beside my bed. There were always make-believe stories on that radio show, such as *Bluebeard, Cinderella,* and *The Beauty and the Beast*; and we made up stories like the ones we heard on the radio. Coming down the stairs and through the doors into the summer bedrooms, we could make grand entrances and dramatic exits. We made up stories about princesses and princes and all kinds of imaginary situations.

We did any kind of scary story we had ever heard, and we heard many wonderful ones on *Let's Pretend.*

I also listened on the radio to early morning country music, which I'm not so crazy about; but there was a program that caught my ear. It was Asher and Little Jimmy. I heard them around 6 o'clock in the morning, staying under the covers so that my parents didn't have to get up on Saturday morning. Once I came down to the kitchen and Eleanora wasn't there; I remember going, "Ouch! Ouch!" across the gravel driveway and out to the green grass where I had a swing set and a sliding board. This was the earliest I'd ever been out by myself. I always needed somebody watching. I crossed through the gravel and up the double row of irises that led to the grape arbor. I wasn't much taller than the irises. I was surrounded by purple and blue.

I remember playing under the grape arbor a lot. One morning, I remember going across to the sliding board and going up the steps and being way up there, looking around, and finally sliding down slowly; and then, there was a big bar of wood, with a seat like a bicycle seat, and you could go up by climbing up and taking hold of the handles, climbing up with one foot, then another, going a little higher with each step. I remember wondering if I could get up on that seat. I did. Then I was there, and it had handles you could hold on to, and I was thinking, "It's wonderful! I am on top of the world all by myself." Then I got a little scared because I didn't know how to go down. Fortunately, Ruth went out to feed her chickens and caught a glimpse of me there and she started singing and coming toward me. She didn't want to scare me. And Ruth got me down. I was so glad to see her, and I heard her voice coming. I was so glad she came to help me down because I wasn't sure I could do it by myself.

The World As I Saw It

I did do a lot of things by myself. I was good at remembering where things were but not so good at seeing insects—like bees all around the hollyhocks. I don't see that well. I only had sight in the left eye.

I had had a glaucoma operation on the right side at Vanderbilt before we moved to Louisville, when I was about two and a half years old, but I never had any sight in the right eye. I was born with cataracts, and the technique for removing cataracts was totally different from what they do now. The idea was that it was done gradually with a little pricking that made the cataract recede a little, and then there would be a little more pricking, and it would recede a little more. Then you'd go back to the doctor, and they would clean it up. The cataract was like a fibrous film on the inside of an egg. They didn't come across people like me very often, and to operate on a child was something nobody wanted to do. But they performed the operation to see if they could open up my eye a little bit better. A mistake was made. They were not able to see the optic nerve on the right side. They knew the one on the left was working, as I could see out of that eye. They really weren't sure whether the other eye was operative at all.

That didn't bother me because I didn't know any of that stuff. I was too young to know. I do remember going to Vanderbilt kicking and screaming, but it really wasn't bad. I don't remember those things as awful. To this day, I put drops in my own eyes and argue with myself about it. I learned at an early age to make a big fuss over anything coming at my eye. It probably wasn't nearly as bad as I thought it was going to be, but I ended up making everyone miserable as much as I could.

Since it didn't work out well at Vanderbilt, I ended up going to an eye, ear, nose, and throat specialist in New York at what must've been a great expense. I loved New York. My grandmother was a pianist and composer, and she was rather well known in New York. So we had tickets to go see *Babes in Toyland.* We sat in the front row. It was like being part of the production. There was lots of dancing and color. It couldn't have been any more wonderful. I got to see it several times because we had to go back to New York a few times.

I was in the hospital and wore bandages off and on. I do remember that I had my very first chicken croquettes in the hospital. They were shaped like upside-down ice-cream cones. They were crunchy on the outside. I couldn't see them, but you don't hesitate to put your hands on things when you're little, so I would feel them and had no trouble at all eating them. The food was delicious, I thought. I felt the whole thing. I knew how tall they were. They were surrounded with chicken gravy. There were green peas floating all around the croquettes. So I have a wonderful picture of them in my mind. It may not have been as wonderful as I pictured it, but I thought it was kind of a magical place. I think I had to stay for five days after each surgery.

I went the first time when I was quite young and returned to New York when I was about seven or eight because the way they did it then was a process. The second time, my father came. He took me for a ride in a hansom cab around Central Park. I couldn't have been over seven or eight because I remember I had leggings that had zippers up the side. I remember Daddy adjusting my hat. He would tie it on under my chin. I knew I had a purple coat because I'd seen it before. The whole thing—the bonnet, the leggings, and the coat—were all purple, and Daddy bought me purple violets. That was one of the first times I had the bandages off. Royalty never felt more royal than I did then!

We went several times to the Russian Tea Room, which had padded gold satin walls, big puffy ones. Waiters would come and bring a tray on a rolling cart. The tray had on it the most delectable things, and you could choose whatever you wanted. I remember going right up to the cart where I could see the tea cakes closely. There were beautiful little cakes with roses on top. I would always eat all around the rose and leave a column of cake under it. Tea was served in silver teapots. Hot chocolate sounded dangerous, so I didn't order that. I had tea instead, and Miss Annie would've been proud because they put cream in it. And I remember going up very close so I could watch the ice skaters, and I believe that was at Radio City. I remember the great anticipation I would feel during the train trip because I knew I would be in New York. Everyone made the surgeries as pleasant as possible, and the nurses were so good. I had a good time.

I'm sure my grandparents helped pay for my surgeries, and that they were very expensive. My father was very young at the time. I've always been so grateful for the parents that I had and my grandparents—I had two sets of grandparents and one great-grandmother who was still alive. I have a gold medallion given to me by my great-grandmother. It has a diamond in the middle and rays coming out from the center. It has her name, Josephine Withers Read, inscribed on it with these words: "Happy birthday Josephine Withers Read, 1854 - 1954, 100 years young." She had two sons, one of whom was my grandfather, Robert. The other son's name was Royal, which was a family name. My husband George took me to Wytheville, Virginia, several times to visit these family members.

On the Sagacity of Animals

I have my great-great-grandfather Robert Enoch Withers' book, *The Autobiography of an Octogenarian*. It was published in 1907, on his 85th birthday. Unfortunately, he died the very day this book was published. I love the picture of him in the frontispiece of this book. It looks exactly like the way you would think a great-great-grandfather would look. Of his twelve children, he had only one son and eleven daughters, including my great-grandmother Josephine. Here is a list of his titles and accomplishments listed on the title page of the book: "Colonel of the Eighteenth Regiment, Virginia Infantry CSA; editor of the *Lynchburg Daily News*; Lieutenant Governor of Virginia; Senator of the United States; Member of the Board of Regents of the Smithsonian Institute; Consul of the United States at Hong Kong; Past Master of the Knights Templar of United States; etc." Our copy has a beautiful marbled paper on the inside of the cover, for which I give my son George credit. This book was read so much that it desperately needed to be re-covered, and George took care of that. I believe we have about three or four copies of it now. I have a picture of Robert Withers from when he was a United States Senator and one of Ingleside, his house which was built in 1869. You can see this picture on Google Earth. His book makes very good reading, although I did not read very carefully all the political ins and outs.

As a child I remember sitting on my father's lap in the wing chair that's now in my room as he read the chapter "On the Sagacity of Animals." I love the way my great-great-grandfather talked about animals. He told so many stories about how smart animals were. He had one dog who followed him to church and always would sleep on the front porch while he went into services. But it was raining one day, and he let the dog come into the church with him.

The dog would lie down just inside the door to the church. Then he would follow him up to the pew, and that was all right as long as he lay down at my great-great-grandfather's feet. But he had to draw the line when the dog got up and followed him up to the communion rail. That was the end of that dog's going to church.

When he was at the University of Virginia Medical School, he remembered every professor and most of the names of the people who were in his classes. He was a great observer. It sounds very stilted now, but I love the way he expressed himself in writing. He wrote this beautiful tribute to his wife, Mary Royal.

> *On 3 February, 1901 we celebrated the fifty-fifth anniversary of our marriage by partaking of an excellent family dinner, no invitations to outsiders having been sent out. We received with pleasure the congratulations and good wishes of children, grandchildren, and great-grandchildren and entered on the fifty-sixth year of married life with every prospect of continued health and happiness. But, alas, these proved fallacious, for within a short time my wife sprained her ankle by falling down a few steps of stairway, and to lessen the pain and swelling, bathed the joint for some time in cold water. This caused her to take cold, which subsequently developed into bronchitis, and though she had the constant attendance of some of the most prominent and skillful physicians of the city, she steadily grew worse until the end came on the second day of March. It would be useless for me to attempt to describe my feelings at this crushing blow. I shall make no effort to do so. For more than half a century, she had held the first place in my thoughts, my esteem, and my affection. She was*

literally the maker of my home, and few men have had a more pleasant one. On her devolved not merely the ordinary obligations of domestic life, but the far more important and responsible duties of rearing, training, and leading her children in the paths of virtue, morality, and religion; and faithfully and efficiently did she discharge them. She was to me a "help meet" in all my trials, a safe counselor in all difficulties, a loving solace in all sorrows. Her disposition was bright and cheerful. Always optimistic, she never yielded to despondency, but, however dark the horizon, could discover the rift in the cloud through which the sun would soon brightly shine. She enjoyed life as much as anyone I ever knew. As proof of this I now recall with much gratification an incident which occurred not more than a month before her fatal illness. The company were discussing that much debated question, whether, permitted again to pass through this earthly pilgrimage, they would pursue the same course or make radical changes in their conduct, and she with much earnestness said, "Well, if I could live my life over again I do not know that I would wish it materially different from what it has been." It was some time before I rallied before the stunning, crushing weight of this great calamity, which was mitigated however by the tender love and affection of my children and the many friends with whom I have been blessed through a long life.

I can't think of a lovelier tribute. I have enormous respect for this man, and though I never knew him in person, my father knew his grandfather very well, and he passed his love for his grandfather on to me in the most genuine way.

I did know his daughter Josephine, my great-grandmother. She had only one leg. She was on crutches all her life. I wear this birthday medal of hers because if I think of fussing about something, it helps me think about her and puts things in perspective. If Daddy's grandmother played a game or performed a task, she did it in spades. She was a crack bridge player. I didn't see the cards well enough so I was excused from playing bridge. Thank goodness for that because I'm sure I would not have lived up to her expectations. I just loved her.

She came to visit us once or twice in Pewee Valley. She went up and down those very steep steps, but I will never know how. She didn't want anybody toadying to her. When it became possible to fly on a commercial airline, she wanted to fly to Florida. She didn't want to go on the train. Going between the cars was kind of awkward. They didn't take people with handicaps. She wrote a letter to the airline requesting that they would make it possible for her to fly to Florida, and they did. I don't know what governor she wrote to or to whom she wrote that letter. She was a very positive person, a person to be reckoned with. She was gracious and lovely, and I was devoted to her, but I probably should've been a little bit afraid of her because she was really emphatic. I don't get that feeling about her father. I guess if you're one of eleven daughters you're going to have to speak up for yourself, and she did.

I was told she was injured on some barbed wire, and her wound became infected. In her late teens, her leg was amputated above the knee. She could swing up and down the steps on that green carpet at my grandfather's home in Evansville, Indiana, when I was about six or eight years old. I have a cousin who is a little bit younger than I, and when we were little, we suggested that she might like to race us. Great-grandmother agreed! And she passed us.

So my great-grandmother defeated me and my cousin Mary Joanne in a race. This was in Evansville, Indiana, where my grandparents lived at 821

Southeast Riverside Drive. Mary Joanne and her mother Josephine, my father's only sister, lived there, so when I went to visit my grandparents, I had the fun of having my cousin living right across the road. Evansville, Indiana, is not a garden spot in my memory. Perhaps it's not fair to Evansville for me to have that kind of opinion.

I'm just enough older than Mary Joanne to have been the first grandchild. Mary Joanne's younger sister Susan would've been a wonderful scribe for the family, but she died young. Mary Jo has a daughter who lives on the West Coast who is a surgeon, so Mary Jo spends more time out West now.

In addition to knowing my grandfather, I also knew his brother Royal, who went off to live in Canada when he was with Westinghouse of Canada. He looked a great deal like my grandfather. I remember going to Wytheville, Virginia, for some vacation, and we were all having breakfast at an inn there, listening to Uncle Royal. To hear him say, "Here here!" was always startling. He had a cross between a Canadian accent and a Virginia accent. I thought it was interesting how so many people have grown up and gone in so many different directions, and still no matter what, somehow or other, they all come together. I had no siblings myself, and that was a good lesson to learn about families. It is what I expect families to do, and I was so happy that it seemed to be working out several generations before. And my great-great-grandfather in that book talks so much about families and gives a good picture of traditions and families progressing.

We are getting ready to have a family picture taken the day after Thanksgiving. I believe thirty-two of us will be in this picture. There may be so many of us that the photographer will have to stand so far back that we won't be able to tell who is who, but I hope the picture is good because it will mean something to everyone in our family, and I will be very glad to have it. I want these children to know their aunts and uncles. I myself had only one aunt, Aunt Josephine, and she and I exchanged letters up until right before she died. I would hope for that sort of relationship for my girls and George. All my girls absolutely adore their brother George. Needless to say, he's the one they yelled at for years. I remember saying to them, "If you all will just calm it down a little bit, you won't believe it, but when you are eighteen years old, you are going to be friends with George." They didn't believe it at the time, but now they are all very close.

Sallie and George, Pebbles and Trucks

George and Sallie were about the same size, and for a time I would dress them in brother-and-sister outfits that matched when we took them to church. I don't think there was any harm in that at all, but maybe it was a sign that I didn't know much about rearing boys. I knew all about girls and what to do with them. I had no knowledge about what little boys thought and what they wanted to do.

I always have in my mind a picture of George and Sallie, and they are two years apart, sitting on the steps of our front porch, at the house we lived in across Old Hickory Boulevard from this house in Middleton Park. Sallie didn't want to go to kindergarten. She didn't want to go off and leave George. They were the only two that didn't give each other a hard time. I remember seeing them sitting there so peacefully, and I expect she saved his life that day.

Sallie was teaching George to count pebbles that day on the porch. George was so little he was learning his ones, twos, and threes. I went in to answer the telephone, and I stayed obviously too long because I talk too much. When I got back, they were not on the porch. I can hear Sallie yelling, "Mama!" as I went down the driveway. She was halfway down the driveway. George was ahead of her. On his little short legs, he was on his way out to the street. I went down to stop them both. She was trying to tell me that he wanted to see the big trucks on Old Hickory Boulevard. Fortunately, there weren't that many then, but it still wasn't safe for a little boy on Old Hickory Boulevard. They got to the gate first. My heart just fell when I arrived at the gate and I saw Sallie sitting on George. But they were all right when I got there. Sallie had George lying on his tummy, and she was sitting on him. She said, "He was too close to the road, and I couldn't stop him, so I knocked him down." And I don't know but what she did save his life. I never did hang on the telephone anymore after that. George wasn't crying really. He was offended because he'd been stopped. He couldn't have been over two and a half years old at that time. He knew what he was going for.

I also remember the time I heard screaming with laughter and great happiness. I went searching for where it came from. We had a guest room in the front and a bathroom that connected with it. I went in that bathroom and found the source. There was a small square tub in there. I pushed the shower curtain back. Sallie and George were both standing in the water and squealing and laughing. If you could bottle that kind of laughing! It was just absolute joy. They had apparently gotten a jar of tadpoles—I don't know when, and I don't know where they had gotten those tadpoles. That was Sallie and George's secret, and they never divulged it to me. They had put this jar of tadpoles in the water. Well, I don't know how long the tadpoles had been in there, perhaps a day or two; and they were turning into what tadpoles turn into. They were jumping and leaping, and those two children were just beside themselves standing in the water with the new baby frogs. This wonderful thing was happening. You could hear the little splashes, followed by George and Sallie's squeals of delight.

There is no way I could convey the joy these two felt in their happy delirium. There was no other word for it. I wasn't that happy because I'm not that good at catching tadpoles that have turned into frogs in my house. I needed somebody from in the kitchen to come help. I don't remember the outcome of this because it was just so unreal. But I had never heard laughter like that, and I never did again. The children were probably three and five at that time. That was one time when I would really have liked to have pictures, though not even pictures would capture the kind of joy that the children were having in that experience.. They had fun, real joy. These kids can't say they never had a wonderful time.

Over the years, all of my children have helped each other through and kept each other safe. And they have shared the joy of living with each other and have increased now to the thirty-two who will come together at my house this Thanksgiving weekend. They still laugh together, though they have moved on to other wells of delight than that tubful of new frogs. Now it's more about the antics and adventures of their children and grandchildren, but it's all connected.

I will tell you soon how this wonderful family came to be, but first, a few words on my school years.

November 2, 2015

CHAPTER II
My Education

Louisville Collegiate School

I started going to the Louisville Collegiate School in the fourth grade, when I was nine years old.

I hope I can find words to help people picture what a wonderful little school it was. The classes were very small. We wore navy-blue pleated skirts and white blouses with big sailor collars and a little tie that hung down about halfway to our knees. I remember many of my classmates and kept up with them for quite a while. Fellow students Glenn Dena Babcock, Susan Speed, and Caroline Dabney come to mind, as well as Susan Mary Madding and Corita Ackerly. I might miss two or three.

During my first year, a tall young woman named Miss Stump taught there. She wore the same uniform that we did. She could read magnificently! That was the beauty of the school. We always listened and were taught how to listen. Miss Stump read to us "The Ballad of the Harp Weaver" by Edna St. Vincent Millay and had us all crying at the end of it. If you'd close your eyes, you wouldn't believe it was the same person reading. That was the kind of reader she was.

The headmistress of the lower school was Mrs. Earl, a tiny, very English lady with gray hair who did not wear the uniform. Sometimes we would be invited to her office where we would sit on the floor and she would read to us, and it was magic. She wasn't the same as Miss Stump, but we all listened carefully to hear every word. I had been read to all my life, but that accent, combined with her soft voice, which I had to lean forward to hear, was miraculous to me.

We sat on the floor. We knitted. We made squares for "Bundles for Britain." Eventually our squares were all put together by some kind soul, and then the completed blanket that we had made was sent to England. We felt very good that we were contributing. We were doing this during World War II as Britain was being bombed in 1940-41. We were right on the edge of our seats all the time, listening to the news in the morning and in the evening. We were very much a part of it. And of course, Mrs. Earl was very English. She encouraged us to be aware of what was going on. We felt responsible for doing our part.

Some of us had parents who signed up and had gone to war. My own father tried to enlist in the Navy. He was turned down for some physical reason and also because he had not had as much advanced mathematics as they required for the Navy. I remember seeing my father come home very depressed one night. My mother explained to me later (but not at the time) that he had been trying to enlist in the Navy and was not accepted. He would not have been too old either. He was born in 1905; my mother was born in 1910.

Louisville Collegiate was a very athletic school. We were responsible for writing our own health record every morning when we came into school. We would write how many hours of sleep we had had, what we had eaten, and what exercise we had gotten the day before. We played tennis. And we played kickball, which was played with rules similar to baseball, but I didn't see well enough to play some of those sports. I could use the tennis ball and a racket and hit it against a backboard because the backboard was dark, and I could see it to some extent. I couldn't be on the opposite side of someone on a tennis court because that person would be too far away for me to see, so I couldn't play that sport. But I was given a racket and ball and told to hit against the backboard, and so that was what I did.

We were divided into two clubs, and everybody was either blue or gold. We were given points for the reports we wrote every morning, and all those points were added up for each team. Graduation awards were given to the team that had the most points. This was serious stuff. I could run pretty well, not counting the stitch in my side. There was nothing wrong with me, but I always seemed to get this pain in my left side. I could participate in nearly all the running games, or they made some kind of adjustment for me so that I could contribute somehow. All that was part of Collegiate, and it was serious and fun at the same time.

We were to be courteous to one another. My big claim to fame was that at the end of the school year, when prizes were given, I won the courtesy tray, a silver tray. Apparently I was polite enough to suit everybody. My mother was inordinately proud of that, because I was not going to bring home any trophies for any kind of physical achievement. But she thought that one was just lovely. I was overwhelmed when I had to get up and walk up on stage to accept that award. Everybody applauded for me! I'll never forget that. I have never had an occasion that thrilled me more. I wasn't going to get any more awards.

Collegiate was a wonderful school. The story was that if you graduated from Collegiate, you could get automatic entrance into Sarah Lawrence College, but I didn't stay long enough to find out. In the summer after I completed sixth grade, my father was made assistant treasurer at Alcoa, and we moved to Pittsburgh.

Pittsburgh and Winchester Thurston

My father had already gone to Pittsburgh when we moved. In the fall of 1941, we made the trip in two cars. Eleanora drove one of the cars. My mother drove me, my dog Donnie, and our canary in the other. We spent the night in Cincinnati at the Netherlands Plaza Hotel, a nice hotel with a big fountain. I had Donnie on a leash. Somehow Donnie got away and went straight to the fountain. As an English springer spaniel, Donnie was a water dog. They love water! He had not seen that much water in a long, long time, and he must have thought, "Oh, this is glorious!" He jumped in the fountain and splashed everything all over everywhere and created quite a stir. Mother came in with the birdcage, which is another story; but we must have been quite a picture in the Netherlands Plaza Hotel. We were escorted upstairs as quickly as they could get enough people together to usher us to the elevator quietly. They were happy to bring us our dinner upstairs. It came in a tall warmer with doors. Somebody who was setting up the table didn't close the door quite right, and Donnie managed to ingest an entire steak. The next day, we made it to Pittsburgh without further incident.

I went to an Episcopal school there called Winchester Thurston. We lived in Pittsburgh for about three years. It was very, very cold and very dirty because, after all, it was a mill town.

During the early part of the war, we had air raid drills. My father was an air raid warden. No German bombers ever actually came close to Pittsburgh, but at the time military authorities did think Hitler might want to bomb Pittsburgh because of all the manufacturing that was done there. So the city was prepared for that possibility.

At Winchester Thurston, Donnie went with me to school, as usual. He was a great companion for a young girl in a new city. Having just moved, we were all a little nuts, and Donnie was very important to our family. There were only the three of us, and he was nearly always among us.

When I got to the Winchester Thurston School, they skipped me a grade and put me in the eighth grade. Thanks to Collegiate's emphasis on English and vocabulary, the headmistress with whom I had an interview gave me too much credit, so they put me in way over my head. I never had enough math to catch up well. The classes were small but there were numerous students in my grade. I remember we would sit around a table with six to eight of the students and the teacher would go around the class and ask us questions. I noticed that many of the people loved my southern accent, so I laid it on a little thicker. I had to make the most of what charms I had.

Sometimes, I was the goat. I was known as one who did quite well in English, and one day they got me. I will never forget it. The word was "akin." Each person around the table was asked what it meant but no one knew. So they said "We'll ask Sallie." By the time it was my turn, I could not recall ever having heard of "akin," and I was so embarrassed, since I was supposed to know the answer to most of these things. My stock went down considerably then with that teacher because I could not think how that word could be used. I think I did know that word, but I went blank. I remember that experience to this day.

Winchester was a good growth experience for me because I had to rely on myself and my abilities more than I had before. Nobody there knew me or my family, so they made no allowances for me. They gave me no special attention except for my odd accent, which they thought was so funny. I have to say that our uniforms were the ugliest ones I had ever seen, and I couldn't help being the type of person who cared about such things; but it was probably good for me even to wear an ugly uniform for a while. In Pittsburgh, I learned about being a little more independent, which included learning how to catch buses. I couldn't read the bus routes across the top of the buses, so I had to learn to speak up and ask questions, which is not always easy for a young girl to do.

Pittsburgh was dark. It was icy, it was snowy, and the snow was dirty. It was not beautiful that I ever saw. Today downtown Pittsburgh is lovely, but then the Golden Triangle was black and dirty. I went to school on a bus. This was during rationing, so we didn't have a car that we had easy access to. It was too cold for Eleanora to be with us, so she hied herself back to Nashville, which was very wise. Pittsburgh was very hard on my mother because breathing all the smoke was difficult for her. We had a German lady who came to help my mother. I remember that my mother tried nobly to help this woman learn how to make hot biscuits. She made a fairly decent biscuit, but she made them early in the day so they had plenty of time to cool off by the time we could eat them. We never had a hot biscuit. We didn't have a microwave back then. We couldn't put the biscuits back in the oven with much success because they got tough when we did that. I remember my mother and biscuits and the ongoing battle. This lady was very sweet, but she couldn't understand us and our foreign ways. She had a hard time understanding what my mother would like to have done, and she mostly did things her way, which was the hard way. I remember her on her hands and knees with a dust cloth wiping every step on our staircases. We had a three-story house. She was dedicated to getting every bit of dust and soot out of her house for my mother's sake and because that was the way she cleaned. It never worked very well.

I made two or three friends at Winchester. One was a girl named Caroline. She had long red braids. Another one was Mercedes McSorley, whom we called "Dede." She came down to Nashville when I made my debut and stayed with us for that whole week. I kept up with her for many, many years. She was part of a large Catholic family, so there were several children in her family that went to Winchester. It was known as a pretty good school. The McSorleys had five children, I think. Dede was the oldest.

I loved going to visit her house. It was a big house in a lovely place to go. Dede had a warm family. There were often a couple of nuns visiting in the front hall. We lived in an area called Squirrel Hill, and Dede lived in a place called Inverness Avenue. Mrs. McSorley was a gentle person, gracious enough to let Dede come down to Nashville for my debut years later. Mr. McSorley was very nice, quite courteous, and a little courtly. I loved him. I went to church with Dede a number of times on Saturdays. We were allowed to ride the bus and go to Gimbels and some other stores to shop and have lunch and catch a certain bus by a certain time to get back home again. We didn't deviate from any of that because we didn't want to disappoint anybody. On Saturdays, frequently, we went to church on our way. She went to confession in a lovely big church there. It was all prescribed and lovely and comforting, everything we did. I think that household made more impression on me than I realized at the time.

I learned a lot at Winchester, but Collegiate was better, looking back. The emphasis was on things I really was interested in. At Winchester we would study maps of Germany and maps of France, and we had to know all the cities, and I didn't particularly enjoy it. It was hard to see, and school just wasn't that much fun. I was better oriented toward the emphases at Collegiate. Those were good years on the whole; however, I wanted out of Pittsburgh. That's how I happened to come back to Nashville.

Home to Nashville and Ward Belmont

There was snow on the ground on my thirteenth birthday, May 19, and I was indignant. I remember, after that, lobbying strongly to go back to Nashville. My parents allowed me to move to Nashville, live with my grandparents for the summer, and begin school in the ninth grade at Ward Belmont that fall. Mother may have come with me for a few months, and then returned to Pittsburgh. Both my parents moved back to Nashville a couple of years later, when I was a junior. Until then, I was a boarding student at Ward Belmont. There were about five of us, and I was the youngest. More boarding students came later. They came from Texas, Florida, and other places. The two-year college drew students more widely, but the high school was less diversified. I didn't attend the college.

I barely got out of high school because I couldn't meet all the requirements to graduate. I couldn't see through a microscope, so that knocked out chemistry, and I couldn't do a lot of biology. I could do part of it, but they were very strict, and they were sorry, but they had their requirements. I couldn't do the whole curriculum. They were extremely pleasant about it, but they had their rules. You understood that they couldn't break the rules for you, and so on.

Now I could write papers and I could read books with a magnifying glass. It took a little bit longer, but I was able to do it. I was quite good in English and in history. At times I had a reader when I was actually in school. I've been read to ever since I was little, and I was a fairly good listener.

I did get a lot of good from going to Ward Belmont. For instance, Mrs. Hay was a remarkable history teacher. She presided over all the junior and senior history courses. I took her English history course. The story was that she donated her brain to Vanderbilt when the time came because she was so intelligent and talented in so many ways. Her desk was on the dais and she sat behind it and filled up the whole space. She had white, white hair, and she pretty much always wore the same black dress. What she talked about, and her enthusiasm for her subject, intrigued me. She particularly caught my interest when she was talking about the royal succession in England. She had a way of convincing you that you were on the scene when she was talking about history and made you wonder whether she had been there when it happened. She described things happening as she saw them, and she made us believe what she was saying. I'm not sure if all the students felt the same, but I certainly did. She helped me develop a great interest in whatever we were studying at the time. I made very good grades in history as a result of her excellent teaching.

They were very generous about giving me a front-row seat. Having a front-row seat was supposed to make it all good. I didn't want to admit it, but I still couldn't see the board. But I felt as though they were making all these concessions for me, and everybody was trying so hard, so I should sit down and shut up. At least that's the way I received it. One comment I never appreciated was "Well, Sallie tries." That's pretty unflattering, but the person who said this meant well. I had to find other interests for myself that were better alternatives to many things that came easily to other people.

I almost didn't get to go through graduation with the class. My diploma didn't say what everybody else's did. I think the administration thought, "Well, it will look good." And I did go through the ceremony. They were stretching the point. While they were trying to decide whether or not I could participate in the ceremony, all my friends were choosing their white dresses and so forth. I was only allowed to stand with my class at graduation at the last minute. I was unable to go to the banquets that the graduates were going to. They were very careful about that sort of thing. I think most of my friends knew I was getting a blank diploma. I've got it somewhere, with many a tear stain on it, most likely. My friends had to know it wasn't a full high-school-graduation diploma. There were no two ways about that. There were too many things that I couldn't fully participate in.

But my mother and Grandmother Herbert and my mother's best friend, Kathryn Hedrick, planned something very exciting around that time, and they included me in it. That was a trip to New Orleans. In fact, I helped pick out the chandelier that now hangs in my living room downstairs, which was one of the things we bought on that trip. It's been over our dining room table before, and it's been in our library in our other house. I must've inherited from my mother a love for shopping, which we both shared on this trip. We went to Royal Street to look for antiques. I had a wonderful time. I remember that my neck was just about broken from leaning back and looking up at all the wonderful chandeliers and other things hanging from the ceiling. I just loved Royal Street.

Mother had an incredible eye. With her pencil, she opened to me the things that I hadn't necessarily been able to see. For instance, she would draw the knee of a table to show me what it was like if she thought I hadn't been able to see it myself. We all loved that trip. We were there for three or four days. My grandmother did a lot of the driving as we came back. I learned from that trip that if one thing doesn't work, then something else might be even better.

My grandmother had hoped that I would be a musician. She looked at my hands and thought I had the hands of a great pianist. My grandmother even gave me a piano! But I'm afraid I disappointed her as a musician. I had music lessons in Pewee Valley. Miss Kate tried valiantly to teach me. I had a recital in which I was to play Liszt's Second Hungarian Rhapsody. I was just awful. She thought the beginning of it was pretty simple and that she could ease me into it, but it was really beyond me.

At one point my grandmother was listening to the piano, and she thought it was sounding sort of funny so she opened up the top of the upright piano and looked in and found that I had put all my doll clothes inside it. I played with dolls until my father was probably completely humiliated. I loved my dolls. I really did. Between dolls and dogs I had great company. One of my favorite dolls was a rag doll. I think she had been a model in the children's shop. She was about the size of a four-month-old, and she was redheaded. I like redheads. I've always liked redheads. I named her Catherine after one of my mother's friends. We kept her forever. I had another one that was a Dutch girl. I'm not sure why I enjoyed her because she wasn't cuddly at all, but she was just very cute. At the Anchorage school in Louisville I had studied Holland, and I remembered that always, so maybe that's why I wanted that Dutch girl doll. I've always had a soft spot for the Netherlands because of that.

I love theater and make-believe. I didn't get make-believe mixed up with reality, I don't think; I hope I didn't. But I've always enjoyed listening to fairy stories and tales and had access to them. My grandmother gave me wonderful books: big, beautiful books. I used to say, "Mother, tell me a pink story." We would sit on her friend's front porch, and she would read me a story. Her friend's mother, Mrs. Annie Fellers Johnston, wrote the Little Colonel books. They were all bound in pink.

Mrs. Johnston was a lovely painter, and mother used to paint with her quite often. I am highly conscious of color and texture, so it is understandable that I enjoyed antiquing and learning about different periods of furniture, design, and architecture. Those things were of interest to my mother and many of her friends, and I just inherited all kinds of interests along those lines. It helped that these interests were tactile. Good carving is a joy to touch, and the quality of fabrics can be felt. I also like china, porcelain in particular. I learned a good deal about it gradually. I care a lot more about what the plate looks like than I do about the food on it. But I'm not opposed to a good meal. I like setting up for a party, for example. I loved having birthday parties for our children and picking up different themes for them.

I learned that if I walk into a room, and the light is ahead of me, I can't see who is in that room. Even if they are facing the light, I usually can't. I didn't see teachers or anybody. But I heard voices and knew them extremely well. I know who's behind me, which a lot of people don't know. For instance, I sometimes would say, "Is so-and-so in the room?" I knew she had come in, but someone would say, "No, she hasn't come in the room yet." And I would say, "Well, I know she's here. I hear her in the hall."

There are drawbacks. If I go to a restaurant for example, I may be sitting at a round table. The people who are facing me are in the shadows because they're in silhouette. I might know who's on the right and left but not who's across the table. And, of course, I can't read lips. That's a real limitation. I was really sorry about that because girls were always whispering to each other, and I never knew what they were saying.

I learned that there were some things I couldn't do, and I discovered the things that I'm good at. I went down various roads that were open to me. So my inability to see as other people could see has, in a way, simplified things for me all my life.

November 9, 2015

CHAPTER III
A Family Thanksgiving

The Cousins

I still can't believe that it all worked out as well as it did. We have always gotten together for Thanksgiving. Everybody comes who can. This year, all six of our children, all twelve grandchildren, and all three great-grandchildren were here. Everybody was together and happy. The children brought about four or five friends who had no place to go or couldn't leave town to go home, and then a couple of people came who lived in Middleton way back when George and I first started building here, when Middleton was opened. It was nice to see them again. The weather was questionable, so we worried about it a little bit, since we were planning on having a family portrait taken the next day. But they were all here for dinner, which was a lovely madhouse.

George asked a blessing standing in the confluence of several different rooms. We had to spread out all over the place because there were so many of us. For our dinner, we had two turkeys and one hen. We had stuffing and sweet potatoes without marshmallows. Some of us have an aversion to marshmallows, but not me! I like marshmallows. Sallie brought a big salad; I think Robin did too. Of course you've got to have rolls. And Judy brought two pumpkin pies and a rum cake. Susanne brought pecan tassies like her own grandmother used to make. And it went on and on. It's my fault; I'm probably the only one who likes pumpkin pie. I can hardly wait to get pumpkin pie, and Judy brought two that were all decorated with trees that she made out of dough. The pies were thick and beautiful. I had at least two pieces. We had anything that anyone ever thought of having. Susan made a big pot of green beans, fixed the way we cook them to death in the South. That's the way her two children, John and Sallie, particularly like them. I can't think of anything that we overlooked.

I felt bad about only one thing. It was the first year I haven't been able to be at least helpful in preparing the meal. Normally I would get out the silver and the plates and set the table. We don't use one table where everybody could be seated. There's no way in the world we could have one that big in this house. When we had Thanksgiving at our former house at Number 10, we set up seven or eight tables. Number 10 was the house that I sold, the one George and I built. We call it by its street number on Middleton Park Lane. As we were getting ready for Thanksgiving, Cleo and I were thinking, "Where is the punch bowl?" We both remembered where it was, but the problem was that we had the wrong house in mind. We do that all the time, and she gets the back stairs here mixed up with the one at the other house.

In the middle of dinner, some of the family members changed tables so they could mix and see everybody, and they had to go to the serving tables over and over. There was much visiting back and forth and hugging and carrying on. We were all so glad to be under the same roof. Even the little children—we don't have but two now—were here. They were handed around a bit to free up the parents and let others get to know them close up.

George's son Thomas, who is almost nine, and his ten-year-old cousin Julia Claire Cooke, from South Carolina, were so glad to see each other again. They usually only get together once a year, and it's either for Thanksgiving or Christmas. They had a lot of catching up to do because a year is a long time to be apart when you're that age.

Susan raised a toast in celebration and thanksgiving that Judy was with us and well. Then she also made announcements about the following day, when we would be reassembling on the front porch for a family portrait photograph.

Everybody came and everybody contributed. They all had such a good time together. "The cousins"—my grandchildren refer to themselves as "the cousins" in that age group—all went out together in the evening to Sarah Talley Roos' house and had much fun until I don't know how late. But all were right here the day after, which had been my request.

Meet the Family

I would like to name everyone in the family, starting with our first daughter, because she is one reason why we were almost hysterical with pleasure. Julia Ann was sick with cancer all year. We've been holding our breath through her treatment. Just a little while before she came to Nashville, she was told that she is now cancer-free. She is not too thrilled because her hair is terribly short. I think she looks terrific. Her features have sharpened a little, but that just makes her look smarter. Her jaw line stands out more. She looks happy and alert, and she feels grand. She's even had a chance to go horseback riding once or twice between getting the "all clear" and coming to Nashville. Getting back to riding certainly made her feel happier.

She has a daughter, Jennifer, who is married to Matt Cooke, and their daughter Julia Claire turns ten this year. They were all here from Columbia, South Carolina. Julia Claire's daddy is a wonderful guy, and we love him dearly. He's quite a hunter. Up until this year, he has always had to be the turkey carver, but we let off him off this time.

The next child is Cathy, who is married to David Obolensky, and they have two daughters. Cathy and David were both here. Their daughters are Natalya, who is married to Aaron Davis, and Octavia Obolensky. Octavia lives in New York, to my sorrow, but she was here like everybody else. Natalya and her husband Aaron have a baby daughter named India. She's one year old, and she had fun. We enjoyed getting to know India really well.

Sallie is the third daughter, Sallie Talley. (Those things happen to you.) She and her husband David Talley have two sons and a daughter: Jason, Read, and Sarah Talley Roos. Read and his wife, Danielle, have a new baby daughter named Reagan Hicks Talley. Jason and his wife Amy as yet have no children; nor do Sarah and her husband Zachary (Zach).

George is the next child, who is married to Susanne, and their son is Thomas.

The next daughter is Susan. (All these are named for grandparents, but I won't go into that. If I get off track, I might leave somebody out!) She's Susan Hicks Thetford, with a son, John, and a daughter, Sallie. (I'm afraid we're stuck with naming children that way for generations.) John is about to be engaged but nobody knows until he asks permission of her father. Sarah Stringfellow will be the one. I love the last name Stringfellow. It's so English I can't stand it! We know Sarah, and we love her, but John has to go to her family's home in Memphis this weekend and ask permission of her father. I don't think it will be a problem. John's already practically part of their family. Sarah has several brothers, and John's been involved in two of their weddings. But still, he hasn't spoken to the father yet, so that has to be done.

The last daughter is Robin. We weren't going to get more boys apparently, so she's named for my father, whose name was Robert Read. That's as close as I could get. We had a cook named Roberta so we couldn't quite name her that. Robin was the best that I could do. I used to worry that she would mind being a sixty-year-old Robin, but she likes her name just fine. I didn't know a single Robin in that generation, so I worried about naming her that, but I was determined that Daddy was going to get a namesake somewhere down the line.

Robin has one daughter, Rachael, and one son, McClain, from her first marriage. Their last name is Porter. Rachael, who is about a year and a half older than her brother McClain, has come back to Nashville to work with her mother in the real estate business. They did a good deal of growing up out west because that's where their father, Robin's former husband, took them quite often. They've benefited a great deal from the time spent in the West, but they turned into Southerners again, and they're grateful and happy to be back home. McClain is twenty-four, I think, and is just getting into an extraordinary business that is going to be in Kentucky. At about six feet two, he is close to being as tall as his grandfather Hicks. McClain was quite a great skier, but not just simple skiing. He did the flip-flop variety. There's a name for it and I don't remember what it is. He did some exhibition skiing professionally out west. Now he's gotten involved in a business that he kind of thought up. He's interested in nature and in utilizing it well. He picked that up when he was in college in Idaho and has a good deal of training. He's sweet, gentle, independent—just a delightful young man. I have enormous affection for him.

Robin's son by her second marriage is Gustav Dahl. He leaves Sunday to be in Ireland for three months. He's a horse trainer, a rider, and an extraordinary young man. This will be his second winter in Ireland during the training season. Gus must be twenty. He's very young to be a professional trainer and rider. I spent some time worrying about it, but on the other hand he's very competent, and he's been in the saddle since he was a very young child. He will be back for the Steeplechase next spring.

He rode in the big race of the Steeplechase last spring. That was his first time in the big race. He rode a local horse, a U.S. horse in this case, and he did extremely well. For much of the race he was in first place. We all turn out to watch Gus. Until recently, I went to the Steeplechase every year. It's just out the gate and down the road a little distance from our house. It's an exciting race that requires jumping over hedges and fences. We feel as though it is practically in our back yard. I couldn't go last spring. I can't walk the distance up the hill and to our box any more. But there have always been a lot of Hickses to fill our box. This is something we've done since we were Pony Clubbers, and that goes back to when the girls were six, seven, and eight years old.

I think that's everybody.

A Family Portrait

I was so jubilant over the weekend because everybody, absolutely everybody, was here. It was for a short period, but they were here. I saw the gathering on the day after Thanksgiving as a tribute to my husband George and the tremendous family that he gave us. I was so happy to have everybody here together and so happy that they seemed to be so close. I can't think of anything that makes me happier.

Susan asked a photographer to come to my house to meet the whole family and make a portrait the next morning at 11:00 a.m. Everybody came promptly, including the babies. They put a chair on the porch for me to sit in, and everyone was placed appropriately all around me. I can't wait to see that picture. Then they broke up into the families for more portraits.

It was unreal, being there with all of my family. I was almost dizzy with joy. I think back to how we started, and I can hardly believe that all of a sudden I am sitting there in the middle of that tremendous family. I can't believe the child that I know myself to be, and it's been this long, and here we are. To me it's miraculous.

The interesting thing is that I see George's qualities so much in each one of them. It is almost eerie. I see his tenacity, kindness, and quiet determination in each one of them. They're very attuned to how each one is getting along. When Judy was so sick all this past year, they didn't make a big deal over it, but they have called and talked to her and to her daughter Jennifer. Because of her degrees and background in law and nursing, she's called on to be an expert witness in medical cases. She is an education nut, but she's so quiet about it.

Jennifer quietly wrote down everything that went on with Judy's doctors, every move that was made. I couldn't be there or help out in any way, but Jennifer followed everything and kept me up to date with what was going on during the scary parts. I knew she was right there, and she had the expertise and the wisdom to watch for everything. Judy's treatment went wrong once, and Jennifer got onto it immediately. Everybody hove to a little better than they might have if she hadn't been there. She was with her mother constantly all the way through.

Jennifer and Matt both graduated from Sewanee, and then they went on to the University of South Carolina. Matt went on to more school. He is educated to the hilt in some kind of studies about the earth. He's done a lot of research on where it would be safe to put certain types of installations. He's a big, handsome, tall, happy, congenial person. I think Julia Claire is showing signs of being a good little tennis player, and I think Matt is (deservedly) taking a little credit for that. When she was a baby sitting on the floor, he used to roll balls back and forth to her. She would watch and learn hand-eye coordination. What he taught her is showing itself now. He's a wonderful, big daddy for a little girl, and they're very congenial, very close. They have a great little family.

Looking around me as the photographs were being taken, it was almost unbelievable to me that we were all here. All the babies were well. Everybody was together. Everybody was having a good time. Everybody felt a little bit the way I did, I think. It was almost too beautiful to me that we were all together. I imagined talking to the father of this whole family, to George. "Can you believe that this is the way it is?" It seemed quite beyond anything that I would have imagined. He and I created so many memories with our family when he was with us, and now so many of these rushed back to me, and he was with us in them all. I had the feeling that he knew we were all there and all were well, and that he was saying, "It's all right. Everything's all right."

I was talking to God a lot, too. I don't understand how he can hear everybody at once. But apparently he likes it when people pray. I sure gave him an earful that day. We pulled an awful lot of happiness out.

This moment was the fulfillment of a lifetime of care and love for our children and their growing families. It was the answering of all the prayers I had ever offered for safe returns home after trips, for help through problems, for healing from illness and disease. They had been through a lot, but they had come through and they were doing well. I think they looked at each other and thought, "This really is rare; isn't it?" I was floating the rest of the day.

I realize that soon I need to tell the story of how I met the father of all these children. But first, these Thanksgiving memories have stirred up my memory of how we came to build the last house we lived in together.

10 Middleton Park Lane

We'd raised our family across the road on fifty-two acres in a house (designed and built by George) that was big enough for lots of children and their friends; but after Robin married, we decided we wanted to build something different for ourselves which would still accommodate everybody. About that time, in late 1980s, George bought this property across the street on the south side of Old Hickory Boulevard.

It was about twenty-two acres, right next door to the Sensings. The couple who owned it lived in the little house on the property. George saw it was going to be available and knew that a family of about twelve people was going to inherit it. They all wanted to sell it. George bought the farmhouse and the land, and we sold our house and land across the street and up the hill. We made some additions to the farmhouse, updated it, and lived there for several years. When we moved into Number 10, we gave the farmhouse to Cathy and David Obolensky, who still live there. Their daughters, Natalya and Octavia, grew up there.

We began to put together the house in our head. We travelled around through Virginia and some in North Carolina, and also Atlanta. We took pictures of houses and parts of houses that captured the feeling we wanted. When we got home, we showed our pictures to Charlie Warterfield, who was not only a fine architect but also George's golf buddy and a good friend to us both. He looked at some of the pictures and said, "Do you know what you've got? You've not realized it apparently, but you've taken pictures of the Bottomley House." It turned out William Lawrence Bottomley was an eminent architect and builder 100 years ago. The Bottomley House is a stately, elegant house he designed in Richmond, Virginia, which is now owned by the University of Richmond. I didn't realize at the time what a good example we picked for what we wanted our house to be like.

We wanted to build a town house, without a lot of land to take care of. We no longer needed all that land for the ponies and horses. We wanted a very traditional house, a house with good manners, one that would inspire everybody. We needed tall ceilings for George and long vertical lines to please me. We wanted doors that closed to permit privacy, a dining room big enough to have a table for twelve, and lots of fireplaces. I loved the library with the door closed and a fire in the fireplace when it was cold outside.

Eventually, George got the necessary permits to develop the property at Middleton Park. George already had in mind what he wanted to do with it. He saw the large amount of unused property as a development prospect. He thought it was time to build a development this far from town, that this property should be used for fine homes, and that each one would be built in a pure, traditional American architectural style. Nashville was developing in such a way that smaller lots were becoming very desirable. He divided the twenty-two acres into about fifty lots, developed the roads, put in the infrastructure, and prepared to make the lots available.

When the Middleton development was designed, we had no idea whether it would work or not. That kind of development was a fairly different idea for this area. The lots around here at the time were many acres each and well separated from each other, so people weren't used to this kind of neighborhood development. Several of the neighbors were livid. They hated the whole idea. This is a big property, and they wanted it left alone. George had also provoked heated opposition in the 1970s when he developed some one-acre lots on Chickering Road. Now that these lots all have beautiful houses built on them, the entire area George developed is accepted as a beautiful place to live. He'd be amazed that we're completely sold out at Middleton Park. No one complains now.

Along with the development of the other lots came the decision to pick out our lot and build our own house. Charlie Warterfield came over one morning, and he and George went out among the lots and walked and walked and thought and thought. I watched them for three or four hours. They went back in the afternoon for more walking and thinking until they knew which lot the house should go on. Charlie understood the house we were talking about. Working closely with George, Charlie designed the floor plan of what turned out to be exactly the right house.

We had such a good time gathering ideas and inspirations for this house because my love for architecture and design went so well with George's professional experience and skill. We thoroughly enjoyed our trips looking for ideas and examples of what we liked. When we were done, George got to see our dreams made into a home for our family. We finished the house and moved into it in 1991. That was one of the last big joys we had together.

It ended up having a third floor with extra guest-room space up there, so we could accommodate large family gatherings. And we had a fireplace in the library. I loved having a fire in the library when it was cold outside. Not many of the children lived at Number 10, but they all came for special occasions and holidays, and Susan and her children John and Sallie, who were still young back then, lived there until we moved out in 2008.

George cared about doing something well and doing it right. I remember seeing George and a man who worked for him for years and years, Terry Tidwell, down on their hands and knees putting in the circular slate floor in the front hall of Number 10. Drawing the plan for a floor is one thing, but fitting it in and having it cut just right is another. Here were these two men, and they're both on hands and knees putting every piece of stone in place. This wasn't just a house to him; it was a work of art, and he put himself into every aspect of its creation.

One of the most amazing features of the house was the staircase. I am sure George and Charlie planned it in such a way that, when the sun comes up in the morning, it spills through the big window at the head of the stairs straight down the steps. Every morning I would call George and say, "Breakfast is ready," and he'd come down the steps and around the corner from the landing and straight down in a shaft of light. Going up at night, when the moon is just right, that same window catches the most incredible shower of silver. It's not stained glass at all, but crystal, which refracts the light in the most interesting way. As you climb the steps at night to go bed about 10:30, you're climbing a silver stairway. The staircase is one of several magic spots that George and Charlie built into the house.

Number 10 Middleton Park has many characteristics that George and Charlie worked out with great care, so it was a living house to us in a lot of ways. I was sorry to give Number 10 up, but when the time was right, I sold it to Mr. and Mrs. Ridley Wills III. I believe I can tell from one thing that they truly appreciate the house. After the Willses bought it, they added very little to it, and they tore out next to nothing, which is very flattering. I appreciate that. That house is George's legacy.

Some of George's Land Development History

George was largely known as a land developer, and you know how awful they are. They just obliterate the countryside. George never built any small houses in Nashville, but he got involved in doing a good bit of development that made people furious. The Bonaventure development on Belle Meade Boulevard was going in at about that time. We had nothing to do with that. It was being built on a wedge of property on the right hand side as you go toward the Club from Harding Road, and some other bad land developer bought it and divided it into about six or maybe eight lots. It has a nice gate that you pull through. Today it's accepted as a wonderful place to live. But when that was being worked out, it was contentious. Belle Meade really wouldn't think of developing property that way. They were some of the nicest people in the world, but they could get awfully huffy and upset. And the Middleton Park development caught some of the opposition that had been stirred up with Bonaventure.

Years before, when George wanted to buy that piece of property between Chickering Road and Chancery Lane after it became available, where Herbert Place now is, several people said, "Don't sell it to him; he'll just cut it all up!" Whoever owned it had died, and the bank wanted to sell it to George. He said that he'd really like to have it, but some people who objected dragged him to court. Mr. Webster, Hallie Webster's father, said it ought to be a park. He said, "He'll buy that property over my dead body." And the poor man didn't live more than about another year.

It was awful. The case went to trial. The judge said, "All right, Mr. Webster, would you like to buy it?" No, he didn't want to buy it, but he certainly didn't want Hicks to buy it. The judge said, "Mr. Hicks, would you sell that property to Mr. Webster?" He would. After that, Mr. Webster had to back down a little bit. I could see his side of the matter. He lived in Belle Meade. He had a beautiful house there. He had every reason to care. The judge said, "Well, does anybody else want to buy this land from Mr. Hicks?" Mr. Hicks said he would sell it for what he was going to pay the bank for it. Nobody would step forward to buy it. Anyway, we got to buy it, and then George was off and running.

Herbert Place goes from Chickering Road to Chancery Lane, and Georgian Place is a cul-de-sac off Herbert Place. George put those roads in and sold the lots. It's developed into something very nice now, but you can't believe how furious people got. Right now it looks the way it's always looked to everybody. You've got to be kind of ancient to know that all that was open land and was available. Today we still have open land in the neighborhood; thank goodness for Edwin and Percy Warner Parks.

Ridley Wills II (father of the Ridley Wills III who bought 10 Middleton Park Lane from me) has written several books about Nashville, and he's called me a time or two to ask, "Now how did that street get named? That was George's property. How did you name those streets?" So there's Georgian Place, which I named for George, and Herbert Place—Herbert was my mother's maiden name. I don't think that there are any more that are that personal. Chancery was there, and then it was extended up into the hills. My parents had a house on Crater Hill, which also went up into the hills, but that was not something we developed. And then they ended up with a house on Georgian Place, one that George built for them. Mother's house was beautifully landscaped, rather French, and quiet. The people who have since bought it put a great big window in the front so it doesn't look like the same house. The proportions are wrong now. But they loved the house and that's the important thing. So we had been involved in that kind of thing for many years really.

Justice Out of Court

My son George reminded me of this event recently, so I want to tell it now. This is an occasion when I was rude, but there's a background to it. While he was being treated for an aortic separation problem, my husband George was being sued about a contract dispute. George appeared to be in excellent health, but he had a very serious condition which could have killed him. He thought it was silly that this man would take him to court over a disagreement they could have worked out on their own. And, in fact, they did, soon after this, become very good friends and eventual partners. But at the time, the man hired one of the top real-estate lawyers in town to pursue his case. George showed how seriously he was taking the lawsuit by hiring as his lawyer our daughter Susan's boyfriend, who had just graduated from law school.

The doctors had said it was absolutely obligatory that George have his medication on an exact schedule, so I was watching my clock; and as the trial rambled on and on, the time came for George to take his medicine. I felt I had to interrupt the court, which one never does, except I didn't care. I wanted to be sure that George took this medicine. It wouldn't take a minute, but he had to have it. The lawyer on the other side objected to the interruption, but the judge allowed George to take his medicine, and we got away with it.

Once before, when we had had to ask to change a court date for medical reasons, that lawyer had insinuated that we were just making up all this medical stuff. It's true that George did look very healthy, but we all knew his status was precarious, and we didn't appreciate these courtroom antics one bit, especially since they seemed to be influencing the judge. And we did lose the case.

Some time after the trial was over, George and I ran into the same lawyer at a social gathering. This was a real whiz-bang attorney, by the way. He had acted so indifferent to George's health during the trial, and I thought he had even used it against us. But now, as he made an unctuous expression of hope to me that George was going to be all right, it seemed to me that he was showing off. He may have meant to be nice, and that was all there was to it. But I wasn't happy about any of it. So as I told young George later, I said, "I accept your apology in the spirit in which you offer it." If he was being sincere, then fine. But I can't see facial expressions very well, and I wasn't so sure. Young George said he felt that was very diplomatic of me, that it was perfect. I suppose he appreciates the way his mom stood up for his dad. That's what a good son does.

A Dream of Peonies

I have been stirring up so many memories lately that one even came to me in a dream. Way back when we lived in Pewee Valley, when I was about four, I had brought a bouquet of peonies into the kitchen so Eleanora could put it in a vase for my mother, who was having some ladies over for lunch. Peonies open up in May, the month of my birthday, so I thought they opened for me. Eleanora put them in a vase and I said, "Let's put them on the table," and we did. They were big, beautiful, puffy, pink ones. As the ladies came in, I was sent upstairs, I'm sure. But I remember there was a big to do about it and lots of laughter and so on. As it turned out, I didn't know, and Eleanora didn't know, that you have to dip peonies in water upside down to kill the ants off. The table was beautiful. And it was also alive with ants. They had crawled all over. I heard Mother's friends laughing and saying, "Oh, but wasn't that sweet!"

I was so embarrassed that I had messed up mother's luncheon. I was upset until Mother explained to me that the party was much livelier than it would have been because of the little surprise that came with the beautiful peonies. My mother had the grace to see the humor in the ant invasion, and she didn't blame me one bit. That made me feel much better about the whole thing, but I did learn something. I love peonies dearly, but I now know you have to give them a good baptism before you bring them inside.

The peonies remind me of another memory that is getting pretty old now. George knew I loved flowers, and every day in the spring, when he would make the quarter-mile trek down the driveway to get the paper at our Old Hickory house, on the way back he would collect the daffodils that bloomed along the driveway. He would walk in the door with the newspaper and an armful of upside-down daffodils, which he would hand me to put in a vase. Through all the years and changes, he was still the man he was in our courtship, which I will tell you about now.

November 30, 2015

CHAPTER IV
Courtship

Chicken Pox Matchmaking

This might be as good a time as any to tell the story of how I met the father of all these children. It was chicken pox. We met because of chicken pox.

The way that we dated way back then is hard for the young people to understand now. Groups of friends who knew each other might be invited to a party. The hostess chose who came and worked out the dates for them. She knew whom she wanted at her party. So she made the choice, and you might get an invitation in the mail that would say, in the girl's case, a boy's name on the back. He would have gotten the same invitation with the girl's name on it, and it was up to him to call and set up picking her up to go to that particular party. That just bumfuzzles everybody. Nobody can believe that we did that, but we did it quite often.

I had a date with a good friend. Actually we were going to double-date. Two boys I knew were to pick up two friends and take them to a Christmas party. I got a call from one of the boys telling me that Doug, my date for this weekend party, had been exposed to chicken pox and wouldn't be able to come. One of his nieces or nephews was the culprit. The boy who called said, "But don't worry; I have a friend that is just getting out of the Navy and I want to introduce you anyway, so I'll bring him with me. We'll pick you up." That's the way it worked out. His name was George Hicks.

Our Sweet First Date

We went by his house on West End Avenue to pick him up. Since he had just gotten out of the Navy, and was quite tall, he hadn't been able to get any new clothing that fit. He had taken the second lieutenant's braid and the brass buttons off his Navy suit. Though his suit looked a little unusual, that was the best he could do. We went up his front steps and rang the doorbell, and his mother answered the door and called him. He came out, and as we were introduced, he offered me a candy bar. He was eating one, and he fished out another one and gave it to me. We picked up one of my best friends, who completed our foursome, and we went on to the party. I was thoroughly intimidated because he was older, five years older than I was. I must have been seventeen. It was 1946 when this happened.

We had a very nice time at the party. As we were leaving—you are always never quite ready to go home—the young man who was driving said, "Let's go to the Chocolate Shop," which was over on Franklin Road. We went to have chocolate ice cream, cake, and hot chocolate, which we did not need. We'd been fed well at the party. Just to make the evening complete, I spilled hot chocolate on George. We were sitting in the back seat and somebody moving around hit my arm. So that helped his suit. I thought, "Oh, I'll never see him again." And I wasn't sure I really wanted to. He was so nice; but he was as scary as he could be. He was not just different from the boys that were close to my age; he seemed to come from a different world. After all, he'd been at the war, in the Philippines. I didn't think I'd ever see him again. And he didn't call me for a long time.

Before that next call, I had seen George at another party held by Ann Frederick, who was a good friend of mine. She gave a party for about five or six couples at her house. At one point I opened the door to the kitchen. Ann was sitting on the counter, and George was kissing her. I said, "Oops!" and backed out. There were quite a few of us, about twelve or fourteen, who saw each other regularly in those days and did things together. I would run into George, but he was dating Ann, and I watched and thought about it, but not much. That whole summer we did things in the same groups. Meanwhile, she was leaving in the fall to go to Wellesley.

At the end of the summer, I had a dinner party at my house for about six or eight couples as a going-away party for Ann. We all were going to the airport to see her off. You could do that then. It's no fun going to the airport any more, but it used to be. We went to the airport and got her on the plane. There was much waving and so on as the plane took her off to school.

Then, early in October, I got a phone call, and it was George asking me to the Vanderbilt vs. Kentucky football game. Yes, I like to go to games. I don't see football as well as everybody else does, but I have a great time, and I enjoy it, and I understand how it works. He picked me up. I would have felt kind of bad about going because I thought Ann might not approve. But we did go, and we had a good time.

The weather for the game was pretty miserable, but we enjoyed ourselves. At one point we left and went to his fraternity house during a real horrid blow of rain. At the fraternity house, he tried to introduce me to somebody there, and all of a sudden he went blank and forgot my name. I think he was trying to remember so many people at once that he could hardly think at all. I didn't help. I just stood there and watched him do it.

After we went back to the stadium for the rest of the game, he took me home; but as he was leaving he said, "I'll pick you up about 8:30, if that's okay." I came in and changed clothes, which I was glad to do because of the wet. We did go out afterwards. I don't remember where, but we did. That was our first date.

Time marched on. We began to see each other quite a bit. We talked a lot. He told me about the Philippines and all kinds of things. We talked easily. There were several places here in Nashville where you could dance. I love to dance. He did, too, but he didn't dance well at all. It was not a great fling, but it was fun. Everything we did was quite fun. We liked music a lot, both of us. I was surprised when he told me about one of the things he had enjoyed in Atlanta when he was in the V-12 Program at Georgia Tech studying engineering. This was after he had had one year at Vanderbilt and before he went up to New London, Connecticut, to Officer Training School. Boys in uniform were invited to usher at the concerts, operas, and other events in Atlanta, and in return, they got to attend the performance for free. He could just go and usher for a little while, and then he heard all the music. For the first time, he developed a real sense of pleasure in types of music different from what you would normally hear on the radio. He liked *Aida*; that was one of his very favorites. He loved that entire program and got a great deal out of that ushering experience. It was a great thing to offer the servicemen, to enable them to hear the great music of the world for just a little bit of service as ushers.

He also gave blood, but he did get paid for that. He gave blood as often as he could, but that wasn't just for the money. He had occasion to see how important it was.

You couldn't get a car right after the war. He'd signed up for one, but he didn't get one for about two years. And he also couldn't buy clothes because what was available didn't fit, and he certainly couldn't afford to have anything tailored. Those were snags for people transitioning into civilian life.

The more we went out, the more I got to know him, and the more fun we had. He dated other people; I insisted on it. I didn't want anybody to date me exclusively, though I think he wanted to. But little by little we began to date more seriously and had such a good time. We took his nieces to the Christmas Parade. We did all kinds of things, nothing spectacular, but just spent time together, getting to know each other. We talked a blue streak. I mean, I even let him talk a blue streak. I do, obviously.

Something quite embarrassing happened at Christmas break after George and I had gone to that game in October. I was invited to dinner at Ann Frederick's house. Her father, Paul, during dinner asked, "What's everybody been doing since summer? Well, we all know what Sallie's been doing since summer." He knew I had gone out with George, and he was pretty upset about it on Ann's behalf. I sank down in my chair and wished I could become invisible.

His Arm Was Always There

I don't know what he liked so much about me. I never could quite figure it out. I did listen to him, and he listened to me. It obviously worked. But I really don't know particularly why. As time went on, he began to realize the things I couldn't do. I brought it up fairly often, saying, "Now, remember. I'm sorry; I can't do that." I began to point those things out because he seemed oblivious, and I noticed he understood. He understood that if we were going down some steps, he didn't grab my arm, but his was always there, right next to me where I could put my hand out if I needed to steady myself.

He did things quietly. And he began to tell me things that indicated he probably realized I couldn't see or couldn't see well. And he would tell me things that were funny that I might have missed, but it was never obvious. He didn't talk about what he liked about me, but we talked about what we liked, period.

We enjoyed doing so many things together. We enjoyed movies quite a bit. We drove around a lot and listened to music. I think one of the things we enjoyed most was South Pacific. We certainly didn't collect records until much later. He played golf, as did my father; and my grandfather played golf well for quite a long time; and it pleased me that George played golf. It's a wonderful game which I respect very much.

When his name finally came up on the list to get a car, he got a navy blue Buick, and what a celebration that was! He was learning Nashville all over, and planning, in his own mind, what he wanted to do. He went to work right away with Foster-Creighton Company, a construction contracting company here, and he worked for them till just about the time we married. He was hired to be an estimator, but he also supervised building-construction jobs and did a lot of things he had learned in the Navy. His degree was in civil engineering. I remember he took me to see a cofferdam he was building. I'd never seen a cofferdam; I wasn't sure what it was. But he was very careful to take me to it and explain how it was being built. It is a kind of dam that stops water, but it is down in the ground.

Without a Word

I remember the day George told me who he was without saying a word. We would go to a particular job; maybe it was building a high school or gymnasium or something. We'd get there and things would be going well enough, but then he saw something he thought was being done wrong. Next thing I know he's apologizing, but he's stopping and taking his shoes off and putting on boots and rolling up his trousers, handing me his tie and jacket, and he'd be down in a hole or someplace where something needed to be done. He was showing some man a better way to do what he was supposed to be doing. Usually it would be a man who was thirty or forty or fifty years old, who had been in construction for years. But George knew a better way, and he wanted it done that way. He didn't tell them how to do it. He got in and showed them. Now I respect that a lot. He was very nice talking to people and they were very nice responding to him. Though he was a big man, about six-feet-four, he was young and light and able to get down into any awkward spot. Then he'd come up, put on real shoes again, and we'd go out to dinner. The way he handled himself in situations like this showed me who he was. It was much better to see it for myself.

George's Family

He was an interesting person, over and over again. He told me a lot about his father, whom he had lost when he was about fourteen, so it must have been 1938. He died quite suddenly from a cold that he had caught when he was walking home after supervising a job himself. He had walked home in the rain to his house on Belle Meade Boulevard. He sat down in the living room to read the mail. He caught a cold, which went into his lungs and turned into pneumonia. This was before the sulfa drugs hit the market.

George had an older brother and sister. They were twelve and thirteen years older than he. So he was born late in a sense, and the older brother and sister were not particularly companionable. Later, George's brother came to work for him, which was very hard on the brother. He really hated it. He thought it was degrading to have to work for his little brother. Here's the older brother, six feet tall if he stretches, and here's George, standing six foot four, without trying. It was hard for Charles. Charles thought he was the heir apparent. I never had any trouble with Charles at all. He was lovely to me and I have no complaint whatsoever, but he was a difficult person. He was very bright, but he never quite made things work out the way he wanted them to. But we saw him for years, many years. But that's another whole sequence.

I should indicate that George quoted his father to me in conversation lots of different ways. Obviously he was very close to him. And I'm sure his father, having these two older children, then this little boy, was very close to him. They did lots of things together. They went fishing. And George's father apparently taught him all kinds of things that George would tell me about. "Dad used to say so and so and so and so." Many of his sayings had to do with the importance of having the right attitude. After his father died, his mother collapsed, which I can certainly understand. She sold the house on Belle Meade Boulevard. The funny thing was, without knowing anything, my mother and father looked at that house after we moved back to Nashville. And I remember it so well. They looked at a number of houses. But I remember that one particularly. That was long before I met George. In any case, the way things double back sometimes is a little eerie.

I had a number of people when we were engaged stop me on the street and say, “Oh, I am so sorry you didn’t know George’s father. He was really a remarkable man.” He grew up in Kentucky, graduated from the University of Kentucky, and went into the insurance business. George’s mother grew up in Louisville as part of a large German family, most of whom I knew in time. There were five girls, so he had four aunts, three of whom I knew. Most of them were just precious. There were a number of brothers, too. One was Uncle Richard. George went into business briefly with Uncle Richard, whom I really loved. But that didn’t tell me about George’s father. George was attached to Uncle Richard and built a large subdivision in Louisville with him. They bought a piece of property and divided it in half, and Uncle Dick took half the lots. George took the other half, and we built those. Uncle Richard was a sweet man, a really wonderful man.

George’s father worked for Life and Casualty, who sent him to Mississippi with his new bride. I don’t know how he connected with the people there originally. But his business was doing very well. Many people liked him, and they really wanted him to preach, but he was having none of it. He simply would not do it. He became Catholic through George’s mother and her big German Catholic family. He was very devoted to his church, but he was not the kind of man that wanted to stand up and preach. As a result, he finally left and went into business for himself, but not in insurance. But that’s where they started. Way before George was thought of, they left Mississippi and came back to Nashville.

High School at Father Ryan

After George's father died, here was this boy left with a mother who was bereft and terribly confused, an older brother Charles who decided he was the heir apparent, and a sister Mary who went to Ward Belmont. George went on to Father Ryan High School. His mother was adamant that he had to go to a Catholic school because that was her background. It was all she knew growing up in Louisville right next door to the church. She was sure that the bishop would be very out of patience if she didn't send him to the Catholic school. In the meantime, on his own he became a Boy Scout and eventually an Eagle Scout. He rode the bus or streetcar or whatever was available to Father Ryan High School and graduated from there. I have to say that when his father died and left this fourteen-year-old boy, the people at Father Ryan were wonderful to him. Several of his teachers took such good care of him and stepped in to be father figures and assistants. They knew his mother was no help through that particular period.

His brother had just finished being expelled from the Coast Guard Academy because he tried to run away with the commandant's daughter. George's father, the year before he died, had to go up and try to get him out of trouble, and Charles didn't behave very well. He was clever; he was funny and bright, but he did things like get his mother to sign his father's car over to him. I guess George was too young to drive at that point anyway. Charles did some sort of fast and not very nice things, and so there was the brother that was behaving badly just before George's father died. Before entering the Coast Guard, he had attended college at Vanderbilt, but he did not stay long enough to graduate because for some unknown reason, he rode his horse up the steps of Kirkland Hall and to the chancellor's office. I don't know whether he had been summoned there, or if he had gone to make a complaint, which would have been like him; but for whatever reason, he decided to pay a visit to the chancellor on horseback. Unfortunately for him, his manner of making this call did not go over very well with the powers that be at Vanderbilt, and he was summarily kicked out.

The priests and teachers at Father Ryan encouraged George in his classwork, which he performed well. He was bright and they understood that he was under a lot of stress and not getting any help athome. I'm sure George's mother tried in a way, but she had too much going on. I learned all this from him and from priests in later years who told me how much they admired his stability and what he did.

His only problem with Father Ryan was that they didn't offer enough math. Their weakness in the math department always annoyed him. He talked to the bishop about it a number of times. They definitely upgraded the school years later while George was on the board, during the time of Bishop Niedergeses, who served as Bishop of the Diocese of Nashville between 1975 and 1992.

While attending Father Ryan, he tried to make up for their lack of math classes by taking math at Vanderbilt. This was the summer before he took the entrance exam for the Naval Academy. As it turned out, he was first runner-up for an appointment to the Naval Academy at Annapolis. Instead, he went to Officer Training School in New London, Connecticut, and made second lieutenant that way. He put himself in the V-12 Program; so he went to Georgia Tech and signed up for engineering and ultimately served in the South Pacific as a Seabee.

When he lost his father, he had to be independent, because his mother was not capable of helping him. It would have been nice if he could have depended on his older brother, but Charles was too busy being Charles. Whatever George did, he did it alone. He loved golf and got quite good at it in high school without even taking lessons. The summer after his father died, he would spend hours playing golf all by himself. He told our son George that this was how he dealt with his grief.

These are the things I learned about him. That's who he was. He was quiet, but able to speak up for himself. One summer, he and a friend painted his mother's apartments. George's father had owned some apartments, which his mother inherited, and George and two Ryan friends painted those for her because, as the landlord, she was responsible for them. George understood they needed to be done. Philip Thoni was one of the buddies that went with him. They painted all summer. Now George would have seen to it that Phil got some sort of remuneration, but I don't think George was paid. They had to ride the streetcar to get there, carrying buckets of paint. That was one of the things they did one summer when he was about fifteen.

I learned as time went on what a special person he was, little by little, as we talked. When he went to construction jobs, I got to go with him and watch. Maybe we'd be there an hour, or half an hour. If there was a problem that had to be worked out, it might take us two hours. He had to do a lot of driving to cover the work, and there was a lot of time for talking. We listened to a lot of music and we just learned things about each other. That was how I got to know him more than any other way.

Maybe he enjoyed the fact that I wanted to listen to him, and I told him things just as odd as the things he was telling me. We listened patiently to each other, and our interests connected. Not too many people our age were interested in architecture and art and living with integrity as topics of conversation and as subjects worth devoting one's life to. What we cared about together, what we held in common—it mattered. We both liked to have fun, but we also had a serious side to us. This was something I learned more about on the day we were married, which was not a happy day, really, but that was for other reasons. Between us, it was a very happy day. But not for everyone.

December 7, 2015

CHAPTER V
Our Weddings Day

Our Different Church Backgrounds

I believe all young ladies look forward happily to the day of their wedding. I don't believe any young lady is so eager for the day of her wedding ceremony that she would want to do it twice.

On our wedding day, George and I were married twice.

My mother understood George a little bit, maybe a lot, maybe a whole lot, and she accepted him. My father was worried, very worried. He thought I was too young for George, and I was a little too polite to remind him that he was five years older than my mother, the same age difference as there was between George and me. He didn't know George, but he didn't think that George would be able to take good care of me, and he just didn't like the whole idea of our getting married, on top of which, George was Catholic. That upset him terribly; it really did. What he didn't know was what George and I had done with each other about church, but how could he have known? I didn't tell him!

The latter part of the time we were dating, I went to church with George on Christmas and all the special holidays. He went with me to get to know my pastor at Christ Episcopal Church. All my life I had been an Episcopalian. We sat on the floor Sunday afternoons at Christ Church and ate popcorn and talked with Peyton Williams, the rector. We talked about all kinds of things. Peyton got to know George pretty well. We went to church maybe once a week. And I got more and more comfortable with George. I knew who he was because I knew what guided him, and I knew his basic beliefs.

I love the Episcopal Church. I made my first communion at St. James' Church in Pewee Valley when I was, I guess, eight, or maybe nine. I also remember extremely well the day I was confirmed there. Father Robert Board was the rector. If he were alive today, he would be one hundred and four. That little church is still going and I love it dearly.

Sitting in God's Lap

Mother told me that one day in that church when I was very little, too little for me to remember this myself, I took a short nap. After I woke up, she said, "Have you been asleep?" She told me that I said, "I've been sitting in God's lap." I always thought I was. It's a big part of who I am; it may not be exactly clear theologically, but nonetheless, that's a lot of the way I feel.

George understood that my faith was important to me, so he did what a good Catholic wouldn't do, which was to go with me late on Sunday afternoons and sit on the floor, eat popcorn, and enjoy long, long conversations with Peyton Williams. I tried to explain to Mother and Daddy that we were doing that, but my father couldn't hear it. He just thought that if George really cared, he wouldn't put me through all that. I'm putting words in his mouth, but that's kind of the way it went. At the same time he couldn't understand why in the world I would go with George and meet the Roman Catholic bishop, and so on. It was very hard for my father. He and his family had been Episcopalians way back in Virginia and I understood and cared about all of that. It's a shame he didn't have more children because too much was centered on me. There were too many things he thought were going to be too hard for me. That's why he was so unhappy.

Not Alice

On the other side, George's mother was absolutely adamant that George must not marry this girl. She'd picked out somebody else whom I knew well and went to school with and loved. She'd been looking at this family for years, and she had it all figured out. It was Alice Tyne. Alice and I were in the same class, and she had the most beautiful, lilting laugh. It just made you feel good all over to hear Alice laugh. George knew her, but I don't know if he ever dated her. Of course, the Tynes were Roman Catholic. I don't know the history. The grandmother was Mrs. Burch. I don't know for sure, but that immediate family was definitely Catholic and Mom—that's what they called Mother Hicks—had it all figured out. I thought it made sense, except that it wouldn't have worked. I knew Alice and loved her very much, but it wouldn't have worked. They were just too different.

Our Two Weddings

My marrying George was also hard for my mother, but she rose to the occasion. We had a little wedding at about 3:00 p.m. on Thursday, April 20, 1950, in the living room of our house on Hampton Avenue, with a reception afterwards. The Rev. Peyton Williams did the ceremony, and Mary Ragland sang beautifully. There were about forty or fifty people there. We had a lovely wedding cake and champagne for everybody. After enjoying the reception for a few minutes, we went upstairs to change. Meanwhile, George's plan for our second wedding was about to unfold.

When we left my parents' house at about 4:30 p.m., the police escort George had arranged led us to the airport, where George's mother and sister Mary were waiting for us. They hadn't attended the wedding because they didn't countenance our Episcopal wedding. As we waited for our plane to come, my future sister-in-law got me to sign a document that I paid no attention to that designated her to receive whatever would go to my estate from the airline if the plane went down and I didn't survive. That was the first time I had ever met Mary.

George's mother went with us on the plane to Atlanta. She was bound and determined to get this done, if it had to be this way. Once there, we took a cab straight to the Catholic church George had gone to the whole time he was at Georgia Tech. A very unhappy young priest was assigned to marry us. The Bishop of Nashville and the administration at Father Ryan had spoken in George's favor with the Bishop of Atlanta, so George had help making the arrangements. Still, this young priest looked very nervous, as though marrying this mixed couple in his study for their second wedding in one day was the last thing on earth he ever wanted to be doing. I sat with George's mother at the church while George chatted with the priest before they invited us into the priest's study. I had to struggle to get my ring off because of course I already had it on. I eventually got it off so I could hand it to the priest again. We were married the second time, right there.

Then we took George's mother to dinner. After a lovely wedding night dinner with George's mother, we went to the train station and took the overnight train to Jacksonville, Florida. George very carefully escorted his mother to her berth, but it was on a different car. She was livid, absolutely livid. But most of what happened was out of my sight. I just heard about it from George, who was awfully amused. At one point along the way, George said, "I wonder if we've got enough time to find a rabbi." And I think he really meant it. I heard him ask about one at the desk at our hotel the next day.

We arrived in Jacksonville at about 11:00 a.m. the next day. George's Uncle Fred, who was married to Mom's sister Christine, met us in his car and drove us all to Ponte Vedra, where he was a member of the Ponte Vedra Club. He made it possible for us to stay there on his membership. Mom was in the front seat, and George and I were in the back. When we got there, we went to check in, and the hotel staff brought us a stack of telegrams. Uncle Fred helped us with our luggage, which wasn't much, because we could only stay two days. Mom started to get out. Fred put his hand on her shoulder and said, "No, Catherine. We are not staying." I had never met Uncle Fred before, but I have loved him ever since he drove us to the Ponte Vedra Club for our honeymoon and drove off with George's mother.

The night before, I'll never forget, when we were finally settled in our compartment, George got down on his knees to say his prayers. Seeing that long-legged boy down on his knees after a day like this, and all the things he'd been through, I thought, "You've got to be the most remarkable man in the world." I was so proud of him. I hoped I could learn how to be like him. You don't forget something like that. He was not at all self-conscious. That's who he was, through and through. I was very grateful we'd gotten through all of this and trusted it would be all right. I never questioned, in any way, that this was the person for me, and that we were supposed to be together. I don't know how it worked out that way. I don't know how that kid gave my date chicken pox, but I am so grateful. We had a remarkable life. We really did. It wasn't all easy but there was never any doubt in my mind that this was how it was supposed to be.

That's what my wedding day was like. I can't say it was a happy day; it really wasn't, exactly, because there were too many unhappy people there, and we were still pushing through to get to the other side.

My mother grew to love George considerably. I think Daddy heaved a sigh of, if not relief, resignation anyway. They wanted only the best for me. They really did. You get one little kid and she's not quite the one you had in mind, and you kind of wish it were a boy, but I only wished they knew. Mother knew, I think, but I don't think Daddy ever really knew how blessed I'd been. I know, and I think our children pretty much know. My father only wanted good things, but he wanted them too bad for me. He was too intense. But family meant a great deal to him, and he'd be very pleased to see the way it all worked out. He'd be more than pleased. "Thank heaven" is the way he'd feel.

We've come a long way and made some people unhappy, but in the long run, we did all of it amazingly well.

A Gift from Heaven

George was very gentle, very kind, and stubborn, which is probably a bad word for me to use, but he was determined. He reasoned things out the best he could and did his best with what was available, and I don't know why it worked. I really don't know how he even asked me to go to that wet football game. You wonder why some of these things evolve the way they do. I wasn't fun, really; I wasn't a lot of fun to take out on a date, I'm sure. We laughed a lot, but it really doesn't make sense. He could have found someone else. Certainly, I was never pretty. I was none of the things a boy would dream about by a long shot. But somehow or other it fell into place. I'm sure he didn't understand it either. I don't think either one of us did. Our life together was a gift, a gift that has filled our world with blessings that keep coming. That's the way I felt sitting there in that chair for our family picture the day after Thanksgiving. To think that it all began on such an unhappy day, and that those who loved us so much, our parents, were so unhappy that day! They had no idea what was happening, but we knew, and we were determined to see it through. It has all been a gift from God. Otherwise, I don't think there is any explanation.

I don't think anyone in my family knows this story in detail. I haven't told it this way before. I suppose it's the kind of story that's better read after I'm gone. The children would never imagine that my wedding day could have been as it was. They would never guess I went on my honeymoon with my mother-in-law!

If you skip ahead twenty or thirty years, Mom ended up living with us, and I was with her when she died. I had grown to be very fond of her. I think she was fairly fond of me most of the time. Mom wasn't as miserable living with us as she thought she would be.

After leaving us in Ponte Vedra the day after our wedding, Uncle Fred drove George's mother to see her sister Christine and then took her the next day to take the train back to Nashville. My mother was downtown in Nashville that afternoon and saw Mrs. Hicks, whom she had met, come out of the train station, apparently preparing to catch a bus or something. Mother stopped and offered her a ride, which she accepted. Mother didn't know we'd gone to Atlanta. I had not said anything to her about this part of the plan. All Mother knew was that we were in Ponte Vedra now. She picked up Mom and took her home.

Now, of all the people that would run across each other! I don't know what Mom said to my mother about having been there in Atlanta for a second wedding, but my mother thought that it was kind of funny that she picked her up. She did know that Mom had gone on the plane somewhere with us. My mother was a lady through and through, and she never would have said, "Do you want to explain all that to me or not?"

Later, I told her, "Well, it's a little complicated, but I'll be glad to tell you."

And she said, "Never mind. It's pretty funny anyway." So we let it go at that. I didn't actually plan to tell it now, but this is where my memories took me. It's funny how one thought leads to another.

How Not to Treat a Sprained Ankle

It might help if I gave you some more background details about why my wedding day was not exactly the happiest day in the world. The preamble to it was something that I did that made it difficult for all of us. Of the several restaurants that George and I liked, one was called Sherry's. It was across from the Royal Oaks Apartments, where Kroger is now. We had gone there fairly often. I was notorious because we would order steak for two. I certainly ate my share. I ran across a big yellow menu from there not long ago. A waiter sketched something on the back of it. What was really impressive were the low prices. Oh my, they were very, very shocking to somebody picking up a menu today.

Another place we liked to go after a movie, or a basketball game, or a football game, was a little restaurant at the end of the Royal Oaks

Apartments' driveway. It was owned, I presume, or at least rented, by an Asian couple, who were as nice as they could be. We would stop there for pie and coffee. The man who presided over the place taught us how to use the abacus, which George caught on to much quicker than I did. They were very attractive and interesting people who shared their excitement with us when they were expecting a baby; and when the baby came, we went to greet the baby. One night, after attending a basketball game, we were walking down the sidewalk, with me on the side that touched the grass. A little piece of the sidewalk had broken off, and another piece was about to break off. When I stepped on it, the corner gave way and I sprained my ankle. George could not have seen that coming because until I stepped on it, it didn't break. While we had pie and coffee, I could tell it was swelling, but I didn't say anything about it. He took me home and walked me to the front door. I was hoping he would leave quickly because it really hurt, but I didn't tell him. He left, and I went in the house.

It was late. As I crawled up the steps, Mother said from another room, "Sallie?"

I said, "Yes'm, it's me." Usually the questions were, "How was the game? Did you have a good time?" Scooting up a couple of more stairs, I said, "The game was over and we stopped to have coffee and pie." So she knew I was in. I didn't see Daddy that night. My ankle was really swelling fast, but I was so smart and knew just what to do.

I went right to my bathroom and sat on the edge of my pink bathtub. I turned on the hot water and set my foot in a bathtub of hot water for at least an hour. I kept adding more and more water. By the next morning, it was swollen halfway to my knee. I couldn't use it for quite a while. The doctor came, looked at it, and said, "You have to keep it up, and do not walk on it." So I was stuck in my room.

Mailbox Cherry Pie

George called the next day, and I told him what I had done. He tried to work out a place where we could go where I wouldn't have to walk. That didn't work. My parents said, "No, you can't go anywhere with that leg." About three or four days later, our housekeeper Bertie (whose real name was Roberta Hill) came upstairs and said, "Mr. George called to say he was going to leave something in the mailbox for you and would I watch for it and go get it." She did, and it turned out to be a cherry pie. Even my mother thought that was unique. They eventually decided that George could come and have pie and coffee because I wasn't going anywhere. The rules were that I had to be dressed and sitting on the bed and the door to my room had to be wide open with a proper chair in it just the right distance from the bed. He could come and visit, and Bertie would bring us pie and coffee. He could stay for half an hour, but I needed to have lots of rest with my foot up.

That's really what happened. He came late one afternoon, and Bertie brought a tray up with pie and coffee. He kept an eye on his watch because he said he had promised to stay only half an hour. He promised he wouldn't overtire me. I had been doing nothing but rest, so there wasn't much chance he would exhaust me, but that's the way it was. When he said, "Uh-oh, time's up," he picked up the tray to take down to Bertie. When he picked up the tray, he leaned down and gave me a kiss on the top of my head and went down the steps to the kitchen. I could hear him talking to Bertie. She had a very soft spot for George; she ran into him fairly often.

I heard him stop by the library and speak to my mother and say, "We've been very careful and followed the rules." Then I heard him come in the front hall and go down the front walk and get in the car and drive off. Bertie came with supper a little later and said, "Mr. George left you a note." I remember exactly what it said: "Keep your foot and your chin up, and I'll see you in church." That was all there was, just scribbled on a note from the kitchen.

It was a long time before I could walk or go anywhere. We could use the telephone, though. My parents were very nice about the phone, which was acceptable for us to use because he was at his house and I was at mine. I don't think there was anybody listening. George and I behaved very properly, but my parents could see that I was stuck. It was December, and I was missing all the Christmas parties. Since it was going to take a long time for this thing to heal, they decided that maybe it would be nice for me be taken over to Wytheville, Virginia, where my great-grandmother lived.

I did go to Wytheville, and I have always been grateful that I went, but I wasn't then. I had a chance to visit with my great-grandmother in her eighties. St. John's Episcopal Church came and sang Christmas carols to us, and it was really lovely. There, they always opened Christmas presents at midnight, so we did that. It was a different kind of Christmas, but it was perfectly lovely, and I enjoyed being with my great-grandmother. The man that helped take care of the house there and did all sorts of things—I think his name was Clay—drove me back to Nashville after Christmas. It's not a long trip and I appreciated knowing him. He told me family history I didn't know, all about my great-grandparents, my grandparents, and several cousins. It was an interlude that I look back on and am awfully glad I did it. But at the time, I don't think I was feeling very gracious about it. I didn't want to be away from George, but my family wanted me to have something to do other than pine away and eat pie all December. To them, it would be better if he were busy doing something else and I was gone. I stayed a month.

Finally, the interlude hadn't done what they hoped it would do. For a while, George would take me out for rides in the car, but I knew I wasn't very good company. By the time early spring came, I was better, and George and I kept right on seeing each other. By the way, this ankle still hurts every now and again. It won't let me forget those early days of our courtship.

Daddy's Difficulties with George

One day Daddy had come home, and George and I had been sitting in the library. George got up to leave and as we were at the front door, Daddy came in through the kitchen. He caught us, so to speak, "saying good-bye." He was unhappy and thought that should not happen anymore. He was concerned that I was seeing way too much of George. All those things added up in his mind.

I have to remember that, for Daddy, it was very important that this boy was five years older and had been in the Navy. I don't know what Daddy thought people in the Navy did, but he thought it would have been better if George hadn't come home. As Bertie told me, "Mr. Read says that Mr. George has been halfway around the world and back." It was that "and back" part that bothered him. Bertie was very interested in all of this.

Also, George was Catholic. You have to live in another time and another place to appreciate how that was. Nashville was much, much smaller then. There was a Catholic community here, certainly, quite a large one. In fact, several Catholic girls, including the Cains, went to Ward Belmont where I was, and I knew them. But socially, the Catholic community was not particularly integrated among school-aged young people. They had such huge families. That didn't fit with what Dad thought was desirable for his daughter. He just was not thrilled that, at the age of seventeen, I was dating a six-foot-four inch Catholic Navy veteran five years older than I.

The funny thing was that his great-grandfather had eleven children, all girls and then finally a boy, which may have been the point, but I don't have any idea. Where he had grown up there had been a very large Catholic community, and his family were Episcopalians from way back. When he had gone to school in Indiana, he saw quite large German Catholic families, so maybe he thought of large families being a German custom, which would not have been popular in 1946.

Catholics were separate. He didn't know any Catholics. They weren't involved in his business community. My grandfather's next-door neighbor, however, was a Dr. Cook who was Catholic, and I played with his children a lot. People develop concepts and ideas sometimes from which nothing can dissuade them. He had preconceived ideas that he brought to this situation, and I wasn't going to change them. Being courted by a Catholic was just something he would prefer his daughter not do.

I was almost eighteen. I had invited George to several events at Ward Belmont. If you had a date, you brought him up to the main house and introduced him to the chaperones, which they had back then at every event. You would stop and chat with Mrs. Jackson, and so on. You could walk around on the campus. You had to sign out and have a permission slip if you were going off the campus. This permission slip was not only from the office, but also from your parents. That was not a problem exactly because I was not a boarding student. I was a day student. Day students could invite somebody to come to the parties. About six of us began to know a lot of the same people just because of the way it was when I first met George. My parents suggested several other people I might enjoy having on a date.

George was in the group with us because when he got out of the Navy and came home, he knew some of the people in our group of friends. Once the first introductions were made, he fit right in and started doing fun things with all of us. I invited him to a party at Christmas the year before I sprained my ankle, when he first got home from the Navy. So he had come, and gone, and he kept coming; and they kept thinking I needed to be going to games and things with more people than this tall boy that kept coming up.

Daddy didn't get used to George. Little by little he would see him, and he was a little bit curt with him. Maybe he hoped George would take the hint that he was coming too often. He was a little formal with him. He would say, "Good evening, George." His attitude was probably clear to George. My father was very polite and careful to behave with propriety because he was always courteous to anybody in his house. But he wasn't encouraging at all. Daddy and George didn't talk about things that an older man and a younger man would be apt to talk about, such as the news or sports or whatever men talk about. He didn't pursue friendly small talk at all. There was no question that George understood and was very courteous, too. George had an imposing presence. His mannerisms were more mature. He was giving Daddy what he was getting, I think.

George persisted. He took me with him sometimes when he had a surveying job to do. His sister asked him to survey a lot she had bought in West Meade. Though it was a pretty piece of property, it was on a hill and it had a difficult shape to it, so that it was hard to place a house on it. She wanted him to show her where the house should go. We went out there and walked around on the lot. We both liked to walk and be outdoors.

When you are walking you do a lot of talking, and you get to know each other pretty well. I think we just enjoyed doing the same things together. We got closer than you might with a contemporary. I'm sure it showed. I thought we were being very cool, but little by little I'm pretty sure it was fairly obvious what was going on. For the first time in my life, I was in love. It was a little scary and unpopular with people that I cared the most about.

We talked about all kinds of things that most contemporaries didn't talk about, like what we liked to read or what music we liked, which is why I knew he liked Aida. We talked about the news, such as it was. We didn't have CNN in our ear all the time. Anytime we were in the car, we were listening to the radio. There were several stations here where you could get light or even rather heavier music that we liked as well. We ended up just liking things together. We could go places and sit and have pie and coffee and just talk and talk and meet people. Our relationship deepened. My mother and father were getting very nervous. I was worried about what would happen if George ever went to Daddy eventually and told him we would like to get married. I think that I was unnerved by the reaction he might get from Daddy and my mother; but Mother had very warm feelings for George, and that helped.

Bertie thought George was wonderful. That's the simple truth. She took telephone calls and gave me messages. "Mr. George will be here around 6:30. He wants you to have dinner." That was the kind of message she would pass to me. George teased her and asked, "Are you teaching her to cook?"

My mother opened the door when he came. I could not feel quite as nervous about telling her that George and I were going to the basketball game. Or maybe we were going with a group to a movie, maybe with Albert and Ann Frederick and so and so. Mother kept up with what was going on and she didn't give me the feeling that she didn't approve. She didn't say, "I don't think you had better do that. You've had too many dates with him." In fact, he was there one day and we were standing in our living room looking out the window and Mother told me later, "You know, George looks at you like he's going to eat you." I thought, "Oh, thank you for telling me that." So she was not unaware of what was happening. It built over a number of months, for about a year and a half. Mother understood the cherry pie kind of thing. She was being won over, but she knew that was not the case for my father. The time came when we began to want to plan a wedding.

An Eminently Appropriate Ring

At first, he brought me a ring which I refused. We'd gone to a hayride on Halloween. Before he went overseas to the Philippines, while he was going to Georgia Tech, he had dated a girl in Atlanta named Sue. Her father was a very nice doctor who let George use his car quite a bit. At one point, before George left the states, he gave Sue a ring. When he got back from the Philippines, he realized he had made a mistake. George asked for the ring back, and she gave it to him. He brought her a big, lovely tablecloth. He said, "Whichever one of us gets married first get to keep the tablecloth." They parted as friends. George went back a number of times I think, when he went to Atlanta, but it was just to see the doctor.

George gave me that ring. It was pretty. It had little diamonds in it. But I wouldn't take it. I said, "No, you bought that for somebody else. I think I'd rather have a cigar band." He accepted my answer and understood it very well. Time passed. He brought me a different ring, a beautiful ring that he had gotten at Steiff's, the jeweler's downtown. He had asked the opinion of a lady of sound judgment who worked there. She had a reputation for approving or disapproving of everything appropriately. As he gave me the ring, George told me this lady had said, "This is eminently appropriate." I can't say I was surprised because there had been the other one that I had given back. This was the afternoon when Daddy came in and caught us in a kiss as George was about to leave. It was not the time to show Daddy the ring, so George left.

He came another time to ask for my hand. Daddy told him he thought I was too young, and it would be well if we postponed any ideas like that. Meanwhile, I had the ring. I must have shown it to Mother. I can't believe I didn't. I showed it to several friends. So it was uncomfortable for him. That was sort of the push and pull that went on for quite a while.

We considered that we were engaged from the time he gave me the ring. We married in April. It was an uncomfortable time in my family, though George and I were very happy looking forward to our future together.

I know I need to give credit to Mother because she saw what she saw, and she felt sure that I was going to be in better hands than Daddy thought. I don't think the Catholic part bothered her that much. She had grown up a Methodist, and she had been an Episcopalian with my father for quite a while. Her own wedding had been a little touchy because her father wasn't too thrilled about it. Her father didn't know my father's family, who were from Virginia and Indiana. He thought a Nashvillian would be better. I don't think he would have thought of a Catholic Nashvillian for his daughter or for me. However, my grandfather was crazy about George, more so as he got to know him. He didn't know him much before our wedding, but he was very fond of him later.

A Wedge-Shaped Lot

Before we were married George bought a wedge-shaped lot on Belle Meade Boulevard and started to build us a house, even though people said, "This young whippersnapper can't buy that lot because it's a wedge shape. He can't build a house on a wedge." He sat down and designed a house that worked on the wedge. Mother was fascinated with that. She was clever and adept at solving problems. He showed her the plans, and she made some suggestions for changes. It ended up having a big living room and high ceilings, which George needed, and two bedrooms and two bathrooms and a dining room and kitchen. It all fit on that crazy lot right across from Emmanuel Baptist Church on Belle Meade Boulevard.

George said, "We're not painting this house." My grandfather, whose whole family was in the brick business, thought George was just wonderful because he understood the beauty of brick. We never did paint that house, but it's white now. It's between Cornwall and Sutherland Avenues, which are on either side of that house. It was a one-story, rather contemporary-looking house with a big window in front.

That was the house he brought me home to after our brief honeymoon in Ponte Vedra. That is where we started this wonderful family I was able to celebrate on Thanksgiving weekend, for which I give thanks every day. It all happened because George persisted, just the way I knew he would, because that was who he was.

December 14, 2015

CHAPTER VI
Christmas Recollections

Weddings in the Future

I just got a call from Susan telling me that her son John (Thetford) went down to Memphis to visit Sarah Stringfellow and her family, as he had told me he would, and to ask her father's permission to marry her. The funny thing was that Mr. Stringfellow had said to John, "Well, good, I think I'll take you shooting that day." I hope this bodes well, but I'm not sure. They have come back home now, and Mr. Stringfellow gave the desired response. We're having that whole family come up from Memphis on Saturday, January 10, for a luncheon to celebrate that new addition to the family.

Our youngest daughter Robin has been a widow for about three years, maybe a little more. She's just become engaged to a man who lives in Lexington, Kentucky. He has similar interests to hers, needless to say. We really like this gentleman that Robin has introduced all of us to. His name is Mike Owen. He owns and breeds racehorses. That's the sort of thing Robin loves. She already has a son who is a jockey. Robin and Mike called to talk to me yesterday, and I asked Mike, "How many ladies-in-waiting do you have?" I think he said there were three due this January and three more in February.

So he expects six foals. "Lady-in-waiting" is a horse person's term for a pregnant mare. He knew what I meant.

Last year, the one that came in March, which is rather late, had everybody very nervous. When he finally arrived, they sent me pictures of him right away. He has two white socks and they called him George Two Socks. There is always a big naming to-do when these new colts arrive. We haven't done that kind of thing in a long time. We didn't breed thoroughbreds, but we did have quite a few that George was looking forward to that might have the right conformation and would be good for riding horses. Mike's horses are not saddle horses. They are thoroughbreds for racing. It's been quite a while since I've been watching the yard and various paddocks for new babies arriving. It makes me cry every time I see a new colt born. It's so beautiful. It really is amazing. So now Robin is going to be counting down the months and the weeks for this new batch that she is going to feel very close to.

Growing Up With Ponies

Mares giving birth to babies have been very important to me ever since the girls began to ride. They all ride. I've got a picture of all five of the girls riding. I was proud to see this picture of them and surprised that we had one. They all started out as Pony Clubbers. It all went back to the day that George went to an auction and brought home a truckload of about eight or ten ponies. Little ponies. He turned them all out in the yard and said, "See if any of them are fun to have." He turned them loose to the girls. Some of the ponies weren't fit to keep because they were rambunctious and so on, but some of them turned out to be good little ponies. The oldest girl was somewhere in the neighborhood of ten. And they just loved it. Because they learned how to handle a pony, they weren't afraid of anything or anybody.

I did some riding myself in high school, but not since. All my girls enjoyed riding. Some of them rose pretty far in the Pony Club. The Pony Club has a whole system based on the British Pony Club, which determines the teachings and the expectations placed on the riders. It's a process that involves peer teaching, which involves the young people helping each other learn to go by proper standards.

You are expected to wear the colored felt backing for the levels you have learned through your whole Pony Club experience. You start out as D1s and D2s; then you go up to C; and if you manage to make your B, you've done very well. Probably one out of sixty makes it to A. We had two girls who rode long enough and well enough to go to Cincinnati to be tested to qualify for their A. That's exciting and nerve-racking. It's very demanding but it's wonderful. It was the best experience my daughters had for learning responsibility.

It reshapes your life to have a relationship with a horse. The horse or pony comes first. You learn that when you come home from school, you are not home free. You've still got a pony to look after, and you've got a stall to clean, which is nobody's favorite thing. You've got to clean your tack, and everything has to be in order. If it's pouring down rain, you still have to go to the barn to feed. All my daughters grew up with that kind of responsibility. Nobody backed out. I've seen some people go out the door kind of unhappy, but they did their duty by their ponies and horses. It makes me very proud of them. I think it was a good basic procedure for any person, no matter what you do or where you are. They've all learned it well and carried it through to adulthood. Some of them, because of hay fever, didn't go as far as others, but they all went to the C program. Sallie went to the B and A, and Judy went to B.

My daughters often rode in horse shows. Sallie still rides, and Judy still rides, and her granddaughter rides now, too. It's something that grows more interesting the more you learn. So I do think it's appropriate that Robin, who still rides, has become engaged to a horse owner and breeder. It just fits with what Robin knows about.

When George brought home a truck full of ponies, black-and-white-spotted, all sorts of sizes and shapes, he had no idea what he had started. It was important in one way or another, to various degrees, to each of the girls. Having horses taught them a lot of things I couldn't teach them. Having a horse was wonderful therapy if you were feeling unsure about a test or no matter what was going on. You could always go to the barn. I'm sure that at one time or another, everybody went to the barn and went up in the hayloft and sat and cried. You can vent all kinds of things in a barn. The barn cat will sometimes commiserate with you, and sometimes not. Lots of life lessons are going on there. I have always been very thankful that we were in a spot where we could have horses. If you live in an apartment, it's not going to work, unless your mother drives you to somewhere that has horses. We couldn't have been more blessed. You never know when a funny thing, like that truck coming home with all those ponies, is going to be that important and change your life forever.

Our son George rode for about a year, and he would ride with his sisters in the park, but he was more interested in other sports and didn't participate in riding competitions. As a typical boy, he wasn't particularly interested in procedure and the exact position that you had to ride in. The hunt seat and the seat for very precise work in the arena are very different kinds of seat. The hands are about the same, but posture, feet and legs, all those little things that matter a great deal to a judge, usually go over a boy's head. Boys aren't interested in being that picky. They want to get on and ride.

Family Christmas Memories

Christmas has always been particularly important to our family. We don't stress Santa Claus a great deal, but the girls and George did, naturally, because they were children and that's what their friends at school and everybody else did. We did the same things every year when the children were small. We always went to church on Christmas. When they got older, we went on Christmas Eve, not for the children's program, but for the big, beautiful musical programs. We wouldn't bring the little ones at midnight. We had friends who would ask, "Could we come and babysit while you and George go?" That meant that we were gone from midnight until about 1:30 or 2:00 in the morning. It's quite a sacrifice for friends to do that. We got to tuck our little ones in on Christmas Eve and still got to go to Midnight Mass! As they got older we did basically the same thing, but they matured and we developed the habit of making our family's traditions on Christmas Eve very important to us all. Now there were times when I understood on Christmas Day that some young people of a certain age got up after we were home and in bed and went in to the Christmas tree and opened a thing or two and saw a new Christmas dress or something or other and put it right back the best they could and went right back to bed. There's camaraderie when children are of similar ages, and they pull off things that are very precious to them to remember.

On Christmas Day, we would have my mother and father and my grandmother and George's mother over to our house, and his only sister was sometimes with us. I'm reminded of this with the many years of pictures we have. It was a quiet family time.

The Cousins Share Memories

The day before yesterday, several of the cousins got together. These are my older daughters' children, since George's little boy is only eight and didn't participate. The cousins were telling me things that they remembered doing. They were sharing memories as you always hope they will. Here were three six-foot-tall boys telling me of things that they had done. It made me feel simply fantastic.

Apparently the cousins were all sitting around talking the night before in Sarah's house. (Sarah and her husband Zach Roos bought a darling old house built in 1910. It didn't look very hopeful, but it was sturdy, and they've sweated bullets to repair it. Now everybody loves going to Sarah's house.) Anyway, they were talking, with Read and Jason among them, and one of the older cousins brought up how years ago they used to say, "We're going to put our fifty cents together and we're going to buy Number 10 back." I had no idea what they remembered about our old house. They were old enough when they used to visit there to remember it now, but I didn't know they cared that much. They had said, "Our goal in life is to go in together if we can, and we're going to buy Number 10 back." There was nothing I'd rather hear, because we'd hoped that house would mean something to them, and lo and behold, it turns out that it does. I don't think anything could be more gratifying than that.

They began to talk about Christmases that they remember there and particularly Thanksgivings. There were times when we had three tables of children at our family Thanksgiving celebrations. They remember when they were very small, at the little children's table in the breakfast room. Then they graduated from the kitchen and moved to the big table in the library, while everybody else spilled out into the dining room. It turned out that they were indignant because the dining room was painted pink by the new owners. The color really is not objectionable; it's very pretty. But they thought it was criminal to paint that room pink. The funny things that stick in people's minds, I just love. They were recounting various episodes of things that happened in that house.

I sat and listened to all that was bubbling up among them. Once, McClain and John and one other, Read, I guess, were out in the back garden while their mothers and I were sitting in the living room when a storm came up. Some of them were sunsuit-size, so they were very small, and the storm was very large and frightening. They could see it from a long way off, and when it came up close, suddenly they could feel the high wind. It seemed to them that a tornado was coming after them.

They ran up onto the porch and up to the side doors that came into the back hall. From two feet up it was glass. They were terrified. They started screaming, "Mama, Mama, Grandmamma, open the door! Open the door!" They were too short to reach the door handle. They began pounding on the glass and broke it. It was not a glass plate. It was sort of an inlaid, leaded glass, some ancient piece that George had found and installed. They pounded on it and broke it. It didn't shatter. It all happened so fast.

I remember getting up and going to the door. They were all hugging each other, very nervous. Those little boys are now in their mid-twenties. As they remember it, they escaped a great funnel cloud. The glass could not be repaired, and they felt bad about having broken it, but their terror had given them an experience they would never forget. I remember that I saw them coming and got up to go down the hall to open the door, and they were very excited, saying, "Oh! Oh!" So it was a big performance from their point of view. They escaped heaven knows what. Those are the kinds of things they were talking about.

They were remembering that one day apparently I gave them all a big lecture about what was acceptable and what was not. When a little neighbor boy was visiting, they were playing together on the third floor when I noticed it had gotten kind of loud. I found out that the children, who were still pretty young, were teasing this little boy. He got scared. I went to the steps and opened the door that went to the third floor and listened a bit, and it didn't sound like a nice conversation, so I called them down. They left the child upstairs and came down. We had the lecture at the foot of the steps. From what they remember, and I remember it too, I made it clear, saying, "This kind of behavior will never be acceptable in this house. We do not tease other people! Particularly, I am shocked that you would tease a younger child." The way they were telling the story two nights ago, bolts of lightning could have been coming out of my head. They will forever remember me scolding them. It just hit me as dead wrong, and I meant to make that impression. Apparently, I did. These are my grandchildren, and they weren't used to me getting angry with them about anything, really.

My Childhood Christmas Memories

I have wonderful Christmas memories. I'm the only child of my parents, so there were only three of us. I'm the only grandchild on one side, and the oldest grandchild on the other side. I am spoiled rotten; there's no doubt about it. I knew it at the time, and it was lovely. I didn't have anybody to teach me how to be teased. Poor George had to teach me how. He had to work at that for quite a few years, I'm sure, because I really am spoiled. George had to cope with that and that could not have been easy. I'm well aware of it.

The childhood Christmas traditions I remember most clearly are the ones I have from when we lived in Pewee Valley, Kentucky. I remember going to St. James' Episcopal Church on Christmas Eve, in the late afternoon just after it turned dark. We always went to the children's program, which was unfailingly beautiful. Some children sang, and some were angels. I remember a shepherd that had a sheep with him, but it was actually a dog. He came down the aisle, and up to the altar where he was supposed to be. He was trying to tell the dog to sit, and the dog finally got tired and went to sleep. Little things like that you remember. Mostly I remember candlelight, beautiful candlelight. It was lovely. Father Board always told stories that we understood. There were lots of grandmothers and grandfathers. That little church is still there, and it's one of my very favorite churches. It's almost like remembering a picture. It couldn't have been real, the way I remember it. But George understood it and took me twice to St. James', when we were in Louisville on a visit. He said, "Wouldn't you like to go out to St. James'?"

"I'd love to, thank you." That's where I was really happy.

When we went home from the Christmas Eve service, we had oyster stew out of a big bowl with a lid, which I never saw except at Christmas. With the stew we had oyster crackers, which I love. I remember seeing my father making eggnog. I was given a spoon with a little silver cup that I could spoon the eggnog out with, but mine was not the same as what came out of Daddy's bowl. I also remember how my father would bring me upstairs to go to bed, and my mother would take a break from being the hostess of everyone present to come upstairs and tuck me in on Christmas Eve.

The Christmas tree was never up until I came downstairs Christmas morning. I didn't even see it the night before. Christmas morning was filled with gorgeous light from the tree. It was just wonderful. Presents would be under the tree, and I usually got dolls. At one point when I was a little older, I longed for an electric train. But nobody believed that I meant it. My cousin in Nashville named Patricia had an electric train that went every which way. It was so magical the way it did things with its bells, whistles, lights, and tunnels to go through. I always thought Patricia was the luckiest girl in the world because she had that train. She didn't realize how fortunate she was. I don't remember telling anybody how much I envied Patricia, and I was ashamed to envy her, but I did.

On Christmas morning, we went to the ten o'clock service. Friends came by, and my grandfather from Nashville always came Christmas Eve, but I only remember seeing him Christmas Day when I was a little older. He would take his Christmas present and say, "Oh, wonderful. Just what I wanted." He would put it under his chair, not even opening it. She made sketches of his boxes, wrapping paper, and ribbons.

When I was older, we always said, "This year we're going to give you a fish, a dead fish, and it's going to be under your chair." We teased him about it. It was so much fun to have him come for Christmas, and he liked seeing us then. Mother would meet him at the train, and he would always say, "Better stop at a filling station. I know she's running on fumes." He expected it; if she ever had a full tank, he would be disappointed, I think. Those are the little things I remember. I don't know why, particularly, but this stuck in my memory. Later, my mother and I would sometimes come to Nashville and see my grandmother and grandfather there, again.

Christmas Today

Christmas has changed for us because there are so many families now. It was not the same automatic series of events it used to be. People came and went. They all came on Christmas Day, but not at the same time. They told me to go downstairs and be available whenever they could come. This plan gave them the flexibility they needed to fit everything they were doing into their schedules, and I got to see them all.

Every face I look at, I may not see it as well as somebody else does. But every last one of them is absolutely beautiful to me, including the new ones, not just the new babies, but the new members of the family. We were talking about Sarah and Zach, who surprised me by growing something of a beard. I thought, "Who are you?" Then I realized, "Oh, it's Zach. Thank goodness."

I have a new picture of Reagan, my newest great-granddaughter. Her father, Read Talley, brought me some additional pictures of Reagan, but I haven't had that one before. She's trying to sit up, and she is a few weeks old in that picture. They are all beautiful, each new member that has been added to the family. They are so sweet and so good to me.

They were very careful when they came to put the food in the kitchen and the dining room. There was a lot of movement. They have choreographed this thing so that I get to see everyone for the right amount of time, not too long and not too short. They took turns coming to sit near me if there were lots of people here at the same time.

On Christmas Eve, I was with Cathy and David Obolensky. They have been in Florida for Christmas for the last twenty years, I guess. Usually I see them before Christmas, and I see them afterward. They would take their daughters and their granddaughter to visit with David's mother Claire in Florida through Christmas. So they haven't been at home. They always call and we talk. Unfortunately, Claire died in March, 2015. This is the first year they've been able to be at home for Christmas. David has two sisters. One lives outside Paris, and one lives in the middle of what sounds like Taos, so they don't come home for Christmas. Several of the other cousins were out of town, but they got home by Christmas Day.

This was my first visit at Cathy and David's home in many years. The Obolenskys' house was full of things that I loved, that I knew. Here's why. Way back when we sold the house at Number 10, I got a secretary to come, and all six of the children took turns choosing what they would like to have. One of them wanted a particular painting, and so on down the line. We pretty much got it all on paper. It's all in a little book, and everybody received a copy of the book. There's a page or two of each child's preferences. I didn't think of it as being sad at all to be preparing to divide up all the things that belonged to me and George; I thought it was a good idea. I don't want people being upset over anything, so they took turns and selected what they loved. Sometimes they got what they wanted, and sometimes they didn't. I had a good time dividing up my worldly possessions. Reality is what it is, and I wanted to be sure there wasn't a scramble after I was ready to be planted. It seemed better to do it when everybody could be up front about it and talk about it. I know that different ones particularly were attached to different things, or might be. I wanted them to have happy memories from various things. That's why we did it. It turned out to be quite a nice party.

When I sold the house, some things needed to be distributed anyway, so we had to determine who would get my silver, who wanted the sideboard, different things like that. Sometimes it was appropriate for them to remove a piece of furniture or a decorative piece right then. Getting all this decided took about a week. That was when Cathy asked for, and took with her, several of my favorite things that used to fill our family dining room at Christmas, and that's why I felt so at home when I went to their house for Christmas dinner.

Over the years my mother and I had been collecting crystal trees. The green ones are absolutely not gettable anymore. They weren't rare, but all of a sudden people looked and said, "I don't see any more anywhere." I wrapped them year after year, and put them away carefully. When I would get them out each year, the girls always said, "Oh, the Christmas trees!" Most of them are crystal, but a lot of them have green through them. They really are pretty. I've always used them pretty much in the middle of the table on a mirrored plaque. Some are a couple of feet tall and most of them taper down. So Cathy had the Christmas trees out. When I walked into her living room, they were on the mantle with candles underneath that made light go all through them. It was as if they were saying, "I'm glad to see you again." It was lovely. There were also Christmas trees on the main dining room table.

When I think of the way our dining room table used to look, I always remember the two three-branch candelabras and one five-branch candelabra, which my grandparents gave George and me when we got married. They always lit up our dining-room table. On Christmas Eve, the Obolenskys had one of these on the kitchen table with two single candlesticks. They also used a couple of beautiful silver covered chafing dishes, which used to be my mother's. Seeing these things again after so long made me feel so at home.

Everywhere I looked I saw things that had been a part of many family celebrations. I think we've used those candelabra for a couple of weddings, so they're connected to each of the girls. Candlelight filled the dining room. I particularly like soft lighting around the room from lots and lots of short and tall candles. I see better in soft light. Bright lights overhead blind everybody, particularly me.

It was a beautiful evening with Cathy and David and their future in-laws, the Davises. I know them so much better now than I used to. I happened to be at the end of the table with Ben, the father, and his children. One grandchild, a little boy named Jackson, was there. He's a babe in arms, maybe ten weeks old. It was so nice to have a little boy there. He was so sweet and went right off to sleep the way a good child on Christmas Eve should. About dessert time they rose and went to get coats and went to church. Their mother-in-law was going to keep Jackson. Two year old India was mercifully taken and put to bed at the appropriate time. She was so good, and so happy, and so cute. You have to have somebody that size if you can. It was a perfect evening.

David is not a chef, but he does love to cook. He is very meticulous. He had a gorgeous, big roast beef. We were all waiting for it to be just exactly right, and it was delicious. He had never tried a big roast beef like that before, outside on the grill. It was done to perfection, and he likes things done to perfection. He doesn't want to fall short on anything, and he wears himself out. Nonetheless, we all are the beneficiaries when he does it. That was a different Christmas for me, but a beautiful Christmas.

I am not walking well enough to go to the midnight Christmas Eve service. Neither knee wants to, and bad knees will drop you like that if you are not careful. So I went to church on Christmas Eve afternoon before I went to Cathy and David's. It was what they call the children's mass. But I love those. I went to the Cathedral of the Incarnation. When it was over, Susan brought me home and turned around and went right back to help with Room in the Inn, an outreach ministry for homeless men. Various churches take turns hosting Room in the Inn through the winter. The guests are fed dinner and given a warm, safe place to spend the night. They have a shower and breakfast the next morning and are given a sandwich to take with them for later in the day. The volunteers who serve the men put a lot into it. I am very proud of Susan for doing that. I asked her how many men they had been having. She said, "We usually have about thirty to put to bed." Where they are bedding down is not far from the nave. The church has a sound system that pipes the service down the hall to where the men can see and hear.

We have a beautiful choir now, and I give a lot of credit to our new choirmaster at the Cathedral, Mr. Schoos, who came to us from California within this last year or two. I am sure he has been choirmaster for an Episcopal church. He has wrought a wonderful thing with our choir. We had a fairly good-sized choir, more or less balanced, but the quality of music was "loving hands at home." I grew up with Episcopal services all my life, and I am very spoiled by how good the music was. The cadence, the quality and balance of the voices—it's just different. I am sure that Mr. Schoos must have had the Episcopal Church in his background. I appreciate him so much, and if my penmanship were anything—I've got one finger now that I can't count on too well—I would write him an absolute love letter because I rejoice every time I hear his choir. It took him eight months at least to begin to train the choir and get them balanced and get the timing right. The music is one of the few things I miss from the Episcopal Church.

I'm unusually picky because of what I grew up with. I guess since George died, I haven't been to Sewanee but twice for their Festival of Lessons and Carols. That was something George loved to do, so we went quite often. At the Cathedral, I like the choir being upstairs in the balcony, and the acoustics are very good. I ought to be a little bit ashamed of myself for being so picky, but that's the way it is.

Robin came by with Mike and showed me the engagement ring he had just given her. I told Mike how lovely it was. Then I told him that I could guarantee that "Mrs. Jackson, who approved of the ring George gave me, would certainly have considered that it was imminently appropriate." Then I said, "So, it is all well and good, and God bless you both."

December 28, 2015

CHAPTER VII
A Rose for Courage

Our Trip to Europe, 1992

It's hard to believe another year has started. I called a while ago to make an appointment, and somebody asked me what was my birthday. I heard myself say, "May the nineteenth, 1929." I'm having trouble saying twenty-anything. How can this be? Most of the time I'm accustomed to it, but every now and again it hits home a little harder.

I had a conversation with Judy, who is back in Columbia, South Carolina, now. We have visited back and forth about things we didn't get said and didn't get done when she was here recently for Thanksgiving because everybody wanted to see her. We were laughing about some of the funny things that have happened in the past. Our conversations also refreshed my memory about things I really didn't want to remember that clearly. I am talking about what happened when George and I went to Europe together in the spring of 1992.

This trip was part of a series of events that had begun six years before. George had never had any serious health issues in his entire life, but out of nowhere in 1986, when he was sixty-two, he had a severe pain in his abdomen that turned out to be a massive dissecting thoracic aneurism. It was definitely a life-threatening event, and the doctors wanted to operate right away. But the pain subsided, and when they told him the extent of the operation and that it could leave him paralyzed, he decided to wait it out and just monitor it. At one point I remember our great friend Larry Long, a radiologist and a very good golfer who is married to George's favorite cousin Claire, telling George that if he didn't let the doctors fix this thing, he would probably never be able to play golf again. George said, "I don't care about golf."

My son George always felt that the aneurism had a profound impact on his father, but I think it just brought out a more thoughtful side of him that my son had not seen before. But it did change our life a bit. George slowed down, ate better, and lost weight. We used to take his blood pressure two or three times a day. We also started traveling more than we had ever done before. Of course, all the children had graduated from college by then, and we were freer to do things together. We went to London, including several trips to the theater, and also to Stonehenge. We drove up to New England several times. So our trip to Europe in 1992 fit this new pattern.

We had been planning a trip to Italy for quite some time. Neither George nor I had ever been to Italy, and we both were looking forward to going there immensely. George particularly wanted to visit Pompeii. We were also going to see Venice, Florence, and especially Rome. We both loved architecture, and we had already had a wonderful time exploring the architectural treasures of England. We also were looking forward to the museums. I would have gladly moved into the Victoria and Albert in London; so we were anticipating the museums of Italy with great enthusiasm.

As we made our plans, George decided we should travel in style, so we bought a car in Germany, not just any car, but a white Mercedes-Benz E-Class. Our plan was to fly to Germany, drive the car to Italy, and drive ourselves from place to place according to our own timetable. We were only supposed to pass through Switzerland because it was on the way between Germany and Italy, but we got stuck in Switzerland.

That is where George got sick. Soon, we realized it was quite serious, and I had to tell the whole family. Judy and my son George got busy and made plans to come to where I was, near Lausanne, Switzerland. I don't think, at that point, that George had ever been to Europe. Judy had been to Ireland many times, as well as to England and France.

George had just driven us on Sunday evening to a small, very attractive inn not far from Lausanne. He had gone in to register, and I waited in the car outside. A lady ran out and started talking to me. "Madame..." she began, but she spoke mostly in French, and I could only tell she was flustered, so I went inside. I found George, just as white as he could be, seated in a chair by a table where he had sat after signing the register. He was quite ill. I encouraged him to get upstairs to our room, and I asked for a doctor. Our concierge found a doctor who quickly arrived at our room. He understood enough English to communicate with me, and I could explain that I didn't know what was the matter this time, but that George had had difficulty several years before with an aortic separation. The doctor very kindly stayed with us. I was able to figure out that he was saying, "We need to get to a hospital."

Someone called for an ambulance. With it came some very big, burly men to help take him down. The elevator was about the size of my elevator here at home, which is quite small, too small to use this time. We had to go down the stairway, a very tight circular stairway, with a pallet. George was six-four and these men were considerably shorter, but burly. I remember standing at the top of the steps watching them take him down. I rode with him to the hospital, which was probably thirty miles away or a little further. I went through all that getting him settled before we realized we were in for a siege.

I learned that George's doctor at the hospital there had graduated from Stanford, and she was interested to discover that my son, who was coming to meet us, was also a Stanford graduate, though not in the medical field. That's where it all started, and that's what Judy and I were reminiscing about. Over the next couple of days, I had conferences with about four or five doctors. I can't imagine that my answers to all their questions were adequate. Well, they didn't know exactly what was happening with George, but they were going on what I had been able to tell them about the aortic problems that he had had before.

Word of our situation got back to Nashville very quickly, and I began to get telephone calls from our doctor. Someone from our bank was considerate enough to call to reassure the hospital that we had insurance and the means to pay them for treatment, which was something I learned to appreciate right away. We were well taken care of. I don't know how it happened, but fortunately a few Canadian nurses appeared who did speak English. Most of the nurses in the hospital did not. But everyone tried hard. They were kind and considerate and took awfully good care of us, or certainly of George. They were looking after me on the side. As a special courtesy, they even gave us a place to stay.

There was a complication, as if we didn't have enough, because the little inn where we had first registered had our luggage. Our Mercedes was also back at the inn. I began to ask around if there was any possibility of getting someone who could go to the inn for me and drive the car back to the hospital parking lot.

Joseph, Our Guardian Angel

This is when, I believe, a miracle happened. I was introduced to a man who may have been somehow associated with the hospital, though I don't quite know how. Some of this is vague to me. He was the nicest little gentleman in the world. He understood our plight, that George was terribly ill. I rode with him on Monday back to the inn to get the luggage, pay the bill, and drive the car back. The hospital had made arrangements for us to stay in their accommodations on the hospital property for families of the ill. Everything there is up and down hill. We were on the second floor of these little apartments. Joseph helped us get our luggage back to where we were staying. He was very solicitous. I thanked him and thought I'd never see him again. But he kept checking in to see if there was anything he could do. His family lived with him nearby. I learned that he and his wife had two children, and that his mother-in-law lived with them. He kept checking in with us to be sure there was nothing else we needed. Now he stayed with us through this whole thing. I told him that my son George was coming. I didn't quite know how, but he was coming, and my daughter also. That night, because Joseph had brought all our things to us, I was able to leave the hospital and go straight to the little apartment and get some sleep.

Meanwhile, on Tuesday, there were lots of conferences about what was going on. The chief surgeon—I think he was a thoracic surgeon—was assigned to look over the problem, and I don't think he talked to our doctors in

Nashville. I'm not quite clear about that. The upshot was that they were going to do surgery.

May 27, 1992

The surgery would be for an aneurism of the aortic arch, which we learned later was a reasonably routine event and not nearly as dangerous as the dissecting thoracic aneurism that he had experienced before. It was planned for 7:00 a.m. on Wednesday. The hospital staff was very careful to bring me meals and refreshments on trays. We were in intensive care the whole time. A sweet little lady would bring a small tray of tea and cookies. She only spoke French; my French is so pathetic. I could have spoken Spanish that she would have understood better. Somebody was looking over my shoulder and saying, "There, there." George would be wheeled away and then he'd be back in our little cubicle where they had us. That went on for a day or a day and a half. Then the surgery was definitely felt necessary; they couldn't do without that.

Little George had a chance to talk to his father on the phone on Tuesday night before catching the flight to Lausanne. It was nice that they had that chat, because that was the last time they would have to talk to each other. Little George said his father had sounded strong on the call and had made a self-deprecating joke about not waiting to see the world and go on adventures until you were too old. But the truth is he had made a special effort to sound as well as he did. When little George joined us, he was shocked that so much had happened.

That night I had dinner first in the hospital; then I went up to my room, took a bath, and went to bed to get some rest before the early morning surgery the next day. I got dressed in my clothes, thinking, "I need to get to the hospital very early in the morning." There was a pounding on my door at what must have been 2:00 or 3:00 a.m., and the gentleman said, "Emergency! Emergency! Madame! Madame!" I was able to open the door, grab my pocketbook, and run. The man said, "Hold my hand," because it was downhill, and we were running all the way down to the hospital entrance. I came in and went down the crazy escalator. They came up to me with a tray of tea and said, "Be seated." George had had a heart attack. There was nothing to do but wait. George would not be able to have surgery the next morning. He was not expected to recover.

Soon I was brought back into the room where my husband was. I was allowed to pull a stool close to the bed where I could sit and rub his head. I read the Twenty-Third Psalm, which we both liked very much, and I said the Lord's Prayer for him. I don't know that he could hear me. He moved his hands some, but he gave no sign that he knew I was there. I kept telling myself that on some level, he might know. After a little while, we were moved back into our little golden room. I call it golden, because the yellow curtains and the sunlight coming into the room gave it a gold color, and that's how I remember the room. I sat with him and waited and waited. The nurses were working with him, and they let me sit at the head of the bed with him. He clearly was not doing well.

The Priest in the Flowered Shirt

That afternoon I asked for a priest because that is what George would have wanted. I created something of a stir because I didn't realize until later that it was a holiday. It was the Wednesday before Ascension Day. In parts of Europe Ascension Day is a holiday, and the parties start the day before.

Anyway, the priest arrived in a little while. I was seated in our little cubicle with George, and I was reading the Twenty-Third Psalm when this man opened the curtains, and there stood Father in a Hawaiian shirt, a bright green Hawaiian shirt with bright pink bougainvilleas all over it, and he had his stole. He spoke no English. He obviously understood why I had asked for him. We then went ahead and he did the anointing.

I kept thinking, "This is so awful, but George would think it was funny." And it was funny, it just plain was, and I saw it somehow or other the same way. The priest in the Hawaiian shirt was anointing my husband, and I was thinking in the back of my mind, "This is going to keep me from flying to pieces because it is so funny." The priest left right after he finished anointing George.

The words passed through my mind, "This is really happening. I can't believe this is real, but it is." Everything that we had between us through the years came to me in broken images that flashed by. "This is real. It is really happening." At some point late that afternoon, while I was sitting there with him, I realized he was no longer with me. There were no more breaths, no more heartbeats. I was so glad I had asked for a priest. George would have wanted a priest, even in a Hawaiian shirt. And I was glad for the humor of it all, because that helped ease the sadness and the shock of what was real, so inescapably, excruciatingly real. That was Wednesday, May 27, 1992.

Judy and George Arrive

The next day, Judy flew to Frankfurt on a morning flight and came the rest of the way by train through Geneva. I know it sounds as though I am making this up, but when she crawled into the first available taxi at the train station to meet me at the hospital, the driver turned around in his seat and asked her, "Are you *Heeks*?" It was our friend Joseph, who brought her to the hospital.

A few hours later, little George showed up in the hospital lobby. He told me all about how he got there. He said, "Mom, I was just outside the bus station," having ridden a bus from the airport to Lausanne, "and a man walked up while I was trying to figure out how to get to the hospital and said, 'Are you George Hicks?' I admitted to it, and he said 'I have your mother at the hospital. I know about your father. Come on. I'll take you.' And he did." Now that was Joseph, our guardian angel that kept popping up all these remarkable times. We were all three to stay in the accommodations they had for us.

While it was very comforting for me to have George and Judy there, I felt so bad for them because while I'd been there as things unfolded over the last few days, for them, everything happened all at once. Somehow we helped each other live through the next twelve to twenty-four hours, I suppose. Beyond that point there were arrangements to be made.

There was a time when we were told that we should meet with the gentleman from the funeral home, and that was almost funny, too. He looked like he was out of central casting. He had a black suit on, but it looked a little dusty. He had big leather folios of pictures of caskets and all the choices could have been out of a bad movie. He put forms in front of us to fill out and confronted us with decisions that had to be made. Getting a casket that fit was just about impossible because in Europe, I suppose, people George's size just didn't die.

We felt like laughing. We were tired and shaken by the whole procedure, but we had to make a choice because they had to do something. They didn't know what to do, and we didn't know what to say. Eventually they found an old box somewhere that would work for the time being. Then George was required to take clothes for him, but there was nothing appropriate because all we had were travel clothes. All these minutiae were very important and needed to be done right away.

Then I got a call from friends in Nashville who had friends in Switzerland, in Lausanne actually. We were still in and out of the hospital right there. The friends had just taken a plane back to Lausanne, after being in Nashville all winter, and they wanted to get in touch with us and have us come to their home. Soon we were having a lovely lunch with them somewhere above Lake Geneva, which is where Lausanne is. They were charming and so good to us and very kind. In the meantime George and his new friend Joseph conferred and made a plan to drive the Mercedes to Paris to ship the car back to the United States. All they had to do was change the plans that were already set up. So George was gone part of the time with him. All this swirls in such a way in my mind that I can't exactly remember the sequence of events.

Somewhere also we needed to leave the hospital accommodations and go to a hotel where we had to wait for a while. Of course there was a lot of paperwork which our new friends in Lausanne helped us take care of at headquarters, so to speak. It was much simpler that this had happened at a hospital. I was told that if you were to become ill and die in a hotel, there would be a lot of gendarmerie involved. It would have been much more complicated. People made it as easy as they could, and it still took us almost a week to come home. George finally left. Judy and I were staying at the hotel. When the day came for the trip home, we were trying to travel on the same plane as the body, but we couldn't. We did have reservations and a lot of help, a lot of people I could not possibly have done without, who were so kind. The hospital gave us sort of a little going-away ceremony as we went. They all went out of their way to be lovely, and we could not have had better care or more sympathy or more understanding. Our friend Joseph drove us to the airport. It'd be awful to leave that out.

The Trip Home

When Judy and I walked into the Lausanne airport, which was not very large, we went to a receiving room where a very handsome young man came to the desk and said, "Bonjour, Madame. Your flight has been cancelled." We thought, "Oh, this just fits; doesn't it?"

Eventually they worked out another arrangement, but I kept saying, "Are we sure that we will be travelling with my husband's body?" I don't know whether they didn't understand what I was asking, or they didn't have a good answer. There was a "Don't worry," and lots of pats on the shoulder.

We flew from Lausanne to London, where we had a tight connection to our flight to the United States. I had a little red suitcase along with all the other luggage. When we got off the plane, they were taking all the luggage out. We were to go and catch a bus to another part of the airport, but we couldn't leave until we got all the luggage. I didn't care about it; I'd have been glad to lose it, but there was a woman who was very officiously saying we had to clear all luggage out of the hold of the airplane. My little red suitcase, a makeup case, was the last one off the plane. Time was getting short; we were going to miss the bus, which meant we would miss the plane. We ran, both of us, in the rain. The walkway was under cover most of the way, but part of the way to get on to the bus was in the rain. So we were soaking wet. Judy was carrying everything she could. I was carrying my suitcase and, of course, that little red pesky thing, trying to keep track of the tickets and all the things that we were supposed to have. We got on the bus and finally got to the other part of the airport. I don't know whether we were at Gatwick or Heathrow. We got on the plane as it was revving up. We were wet and flustered, but the seats we were in were ours. We collapsed and slept until we landed in what we thought was New York, but it turned out to be Newark, New Jersey. I never was able to sort that out.

From there, we had to catch a plane for Nashville. We hadn't eaten in quite a while but we were too tired to care. Our next plane connection was also going to be close. The man who was in charge of helping people make arrangements for their connecting flights was having lunch. We kept hearing our flight for Nashville announced over the loudspeaker, and he was having lunch. We stood there watching him behind the glass wall carefully, slowly eating. He knew we were there, he knew every bit of it. We were in agony as he ate very slowly while we watched the minutes pass on the clock above his window. It took him forever to chew that lunch pizza he was having. Finally, he came out to help us, and we got on the plane with about a split second to spare.

Our plane took us first to Atlanta, where we learned that the coffin was too heavy for the flight to Nashville. It may have been lined with lead. Arrangements had to be made for a hearse to take it to Nashville. Judy and I got on one of the last planes they would let fly into Nashville after midnight. We just barely squeaked in. After we got off the plane, as we walked down the concourse, I heard a familiar sound of laughter. I recognized my daughters' voices and Bishop Niedergeses. They had come to meet our plane, which had been delayed and delayed for hours. Never was I so glad to see anybody in my life. Everybody was slaphappy. Judy and I were close to tears most of the way to the baggage claim area. And what a surprise to be greeted by Bishop Niedergeses, standing there with the girls! How sweet, how generous of him! He had taught George at Father Ryan, so they had known each other from way back. He was not a young man by a long shot, and there he was after midnight with my family.

Somehow we got home. That white Mercedes got to Nashville, where I promptly sold it. The last thing I needed was a car of that caliber. My husband would have loved driving it, but a few days were all he got with it.

I had talked to my mother and the girls every day from Switzerland. Mother's caregiver Carolyn told me, "Mrs. Read sat at the dining room table and directed everything." And she did, from Nashville. She saw to it that some special planning was done. She knew whom to call to get anything done. Carolyn said, "Oh, oh, Mrs. Read handled everything." It was early in the spring and people needed to do some things in the garden, and she realized that they could not have brought the coffin up the front steps. They were steep, stone steps, and the railing on either side would have made it very difficult. My mother knew they'd have to go through the garden gate and through the garden and up the better flight of steps and right through the double doors in the back of the house and into the library. She arranged all of that because I wouldn't have had the sense to realize that it was going to be awkward. She arranged with George and the girls the time for the funeral and so on. She knew just what to do, I'm sorry to say, because she had gone through a lot of family funerals.

She was a good guide for the girls. We set a particular time and everybody gathered, and Carolyn saw that everybody had hot chocolate. They all sat around the table and we all talked to each other. She had been with Mother at least four or five years. She was big, lovely, and sweet; she always wore a beautiful white uniform, and she took awfully good care of my mother, who was not very well. She was very proud of Mrs. Read. "Mrs. Read knew just what to do," she told me repeatedly after I got home.

My son George had come back home to make arrangements to receive his father's body. We got home about the same time as the casket arrived. Of course, we couldn't use the Transylvania-style casket that the funeral home in Switzerland had provided, so someone had to go to the funeral home in Nashville to select one that would be more suitable, one big enough for George. I really don't know how all that came together. I didn't have sense enough to take care of it myself. I think I slept for two days after I was home. Judy did as well.

I remember walking in the front door and seeing a big basket on the hall table. I was told, "These came for you." The basket was full of notes, letters, and cards. I took the whole basket upstairs to bed. I began to read them and finally rolled over and went to sleep. There were sweet notes that I appreciated so much. I read and reread them afterwards. I don't know how much was known in Nashville. I know our doctors and the bank knew what had happened, and things that needed to be done were done. I take no credit for it all. Friends did it all.

The funeral was at the Cathedral of the Incarnation, and it was packed. I remember being shocked when I walked in. Bishop Niedergeses was at that funeral as well, assisting at the altar. I had no idea a program had been worked out. I think I had named some pallbearers, but I don't know whether I dreamt that or not. I think I made suggestions in talking to Mother and she passed all that along. It all has a rather unreal quality about it, which probably is true for anybody experiencing something like what happened to us. But people just came and did what was needed, and it was wonderful. So many of George's friends from the University of Tennessee came. The whole Board of Trustees was nice enough to come. They showed up at times when I wouldn't have expected, except I didn't expect any of it. I recognized their faces.

When Sallie was at UT, George had helped start their horse program and had done some work for their agricultural department. We gave them several horses to help them develop their riding program. He and I attended meetings in connection with these interests, so we had gotten to know many of the members of the board. George had done a lot for the University, and the Board of Trustees showed their gratitude by attending his funeral. That was quite a tribute to George and their appreciation of him.

The people that came in and out of our house in those late spring days in 1992 were wonderful. I am not clear about the details, but I felt the love and support from so many friends and family members. Many friends from way back came to the visitation the day before the funeral. Many came afterwards as well. I was glad we were able to host all these visitors in our new house, which George had enjoyed putting together so much, though it was sad he didn't get to live in it longer. He had put so much love, time, effort, and joy into planning and building that house. We had moved in eight or ten months previously, in fall of 1991.

We moved earlier than planned because my mother, who was going to live with us, sold her house almost overnight, which nobody expected, and the buyers wanted to take possession of her house almost immediately. Our house would have been a lot readier if a young man had not driven a nail through a water pipe, causing the kitchen floor to be flooded so badly that the whole floor had to be redone. Other little things were not finished when we moved in, but eventually they all got taken care of. We were not perturbed about these minor details. We never expected anything like what happened.

Also during these days surrounding the funeral, George remembered our friend Joseph had said that his son loved the New York Yankees, so George sent him a cap from that team after he got home. This was the least we could do, considering all he had done for us. I had given him the money I had, with my profuse thanks, but it wasn't much. After I got home, I found a pretty silver box and had it engraved, "To our guardian angel, Joseph" and "May 27, 1992." I sent that to him as a remembrance and a sign of what his support meant to us when we needed so much help, and I didn't know what I was doing.

I remember sitting in the middle of our bed, cross-legged, with that basket full of notes, cards, and letters. I began picking things up willy-nilly. It took me till late the next night before I went through all of them. I felt totally overwhelmed when I read those notes, some of which were from people I really didn't know very well.

The top one was from a friend who said, "You may not be ready for this right away, but I'm going to church every day for the 7:00 a.m. Mass. I'd love to pick you up each morning and take you with me. Give me a call when you're ready. I can wait a long time, or do it right away." She left her telephone number on the bottom of the note. That was the first note I picked up. As soon as I recovered after the funeral, I called her, and we went together every weekday morning for the next three years.

This was Valere Menefee, the former Valere Potter. Her mother was Valere, too, but where they got the name, I don't know. We were sort of convoluted cousins by marriage. Over a period of time we became close. It was an astonishing thing. We went into the Cathedral every morning. She picked me up at 6:15. She has a good sense of humor and we laughed about a lot of things when we could laugh. It was the right thing to do. I'll be thankful to her forever because she showed me I could go right on doing things. You have to put your feet on the floor in the morning at that hour to do it. I thought, "If she can, I can too. Everybody will feel better if I am up and moving." It would have been easy to stay in bed, but because of friends like her, I didn't.

I never asked why anything happens. I may not like what happened, but I'm not prone to ask, "Why me?" I'm not prone to ask anything along that line, and that's a good thing because you waste a lot of time with that. But I did often say the simple prayer, "Help me." I didn't have a lot of confidence or faith that I could go through what I had to go through, but if I was going to have to, then, I thought, "Let's go together."

In all these early mornings that we went, Father Fleming was the celebrant at Mass at the cathedral. He had cancer of the jaw, but he kept on going with tremendous courage and was an inspiration to many. Early in the morning, there would be a small group of people at Mass. Sometime after Father Fleming became ill, he asked Valere to help distribute communion to the people. She had assisted before, and she accepted his request to help again.

After about a year, he asked if I, too, would like to help give out communion. I said, "Oh, Father, I don't think I'm..." I didn't want to say "worthy," though that was the word I meant. "I don't know that I should be doing or even considering this."

Persisting, he said, "I think you'd like to help." What I wanted to say was, "I don't think you should ask me to do this. I've been coming and I'm here, but I don't have the background or the training to do this." The first morning I did step forward and do it, I'm sure my hand was shaking.

Years later, we would go to visit Father at his house next to the cathedral. He was in bed, and we knew he was very ill. We had the host with us. We were standing by his bed saying the opening prayers of the service for communion of the sick. Valere burst into tears and left the room. She's not given to that. She was terribly moved. They'd been friends for many years, I know. He gestured to me to go ahead, and I had to give him communion then. I was more than honored and certainly moved to do so, but I really ought not to have been the one to do that. His hand was so thin and he was so sick, but he patted my hand and that was it. I'll never forget that time with him. I should not have been allowed to give him communion, but it was very kind of him to ask me to. I will always be grateful to have had that privilege.

A Morning Rose

The day after I knew George was gone, I woke up early in the morning, put on my raincoat, and went out the side door of the hospital's guest quarters to look at the new day. I was not good with a camera, but I had one with me this time. The early morning was very wet and very green. Around the corner of the hospital, I saw a fence with a wire mesh over it which supported a vine that was growing there. All of a sudden, right in front of me, stood one big, gorgeous, rich pink rose, a vision of beauty in the cool morning light. The rose captured my whole attention, and as I stood enraptured, I listened to hear if it would tell me anything. It brought me a peace from a world very different from the previous day's world of sickness, death, and loss. It was as if the rose spoke to me, and I talked right back to it. I remember apologizing for being so arrogant, thinking so much of my own self and my own pain and sorrow, but it was not offended. "Everything will be all right. You will be fine," it seemed to say. I took courage from that one single, gorgeous rose, bold as could be, blooming as big as my palm, bursting with life, pouring beauty into the fresh day, warming the cool Swiss morning.

I took a picture of that rose and kept it for years. Somehow or other when we moved the last time, I lost track of it. Someday I hope to find it again.

January 4, 2016

CHAPTER VIII
The Color of Names

Some People Back Away

The way I remember people's names is a color or a shade of a color or something along those lines. I've always been a little embarrassed about it because when I tell people this they say, "What?" Then people begin to back away, and I certainly understand. I remember somebody brought me an article a few years ago from *Psychology Today* about people who have this particular turn of mind, and there's even a long scientific name for it. I don't know where it comes from, but I am comforted to know that there are other people who think this way, too. People tell me that, over the years, I'm pretty much consistent when I say, "I can't think what her name is, but it's purple." I will be told, "Well, that's what you said before."

I suspect it goes way, way back to an ABC book I was given when I was about three years old. It had great big letters in it, and this was one of the few things I was able to look at and read and remember. I think I remembered it from a very young age, so it has all blended together. Color has much to do with how I perceive the world. It gives texture and light and shadow to things I don't see clearly.

A is always yellow, for example. And words that have *A*, like *Davis*, are pretty much yellow. Those other letters also have a color, but blended together, *Davis* is a warm yellow name. *Joseph* is always red, but it's a particular shade of red. Texture has something to do with it, too, and I can't tie that to anything. *Joseph* is always a nice warm, deep-textured red.

Frequently I don't see things written as easily as most people do. I learned to read from flash cards, which have no color. So I attach a color, which I do care about, to some words. I care about color around me as well. My mother was an artist, and I remember her pastel box and the things that she was sketching with. None of this makes a great deal of sense, but it falls into place and is very helpful to me.

Dog Stories

We're a little obsessive about dogs. The first dog in my life is one I have no clear recollection of at all, the dog that my father brought back to my mother before they were married. She lived in a large apartment on Belle Meade Boulevard. It shows that she really loved my dad that she took it so well. The dog he brought her on the train was an eight- or ten-month-old Great Dane puppy. Everybody said that dog had the most beautiful big brown eyes, and so he was referred to as "Ojo." *Ojo* is Spanish for *eyes*. At every stop, my father got out of his compartment and went around to get Ojo out of the place where they kept animals and take him walking.

I have pictures of him sleeping under my baby buggy when I was put out "in the air." It was considered so important for a baby to sleep in the fresh air. Ojo slept under my buggy. My grandmother, who had no reason whatever to have affection for a dog, loved that one. It was something of a challenge when your potential son-in-law brought your still-living-at-home daughter a Great Dane. Nothing in her background prepared her for such an event. She not only forgave him; she loved him for it.

The first dog I remember clearly was Jerry, a Sealyham terrier. Sealyhams were bred in Wales. They look very much like a Scottie, with which we are all familiar, but Jerry, like other Sealyhams, was white, and his ears didn't stand up. They folded down a little. Sealys have a stiff, short tail. They are bred to be around the barn. That was their original purpose. They became quite fashionable actually. Jerry was a character, but then, so are all terriers.

He bit the sewing lady regularly. I don't know why she came. This was out in Pewee Valley, so I was about three and a half or four. The sewing lady would come in and put her sewing basket by her chair next to a table that was set up for her. Jerry would sleep under the chair that my mother was sitting in, and every time this lady would lean over to get something out of her sewing basket, he'd snap at her. He was fussed at, and he was sent out of the room, but he never got over doing it. Mother had to take the sewing lady to have stitches once.

He endured baby bonnets and doll clothes that I would stuff him into, and he let me parade him around in my doll buggy without a cross word. I think he put up with everything from me because my father was the love of his life. He said to Jerry, "Take care of her." Maybe Jerry didn't like it, but he endured it. I remember Jerry very well because he endured so much from me. He never snapped at me. He never offered to be the least bit grumpy at me.

When Daddy came home, Jerry's world changed completely. He would sit by my father's chair when he was home in the evening before dinner. He would watch Daddy, and Daddy always gave him a piece of ice out of his drink before dinner. He sat and waited for it and waited for it. It was as regular as clockwork. During dinner, he slept under Daddy's chair except when grace was said, when he sat on his hind end. Then Daddy would excuse him, and Jerry would go back under his chair and go to sleep.

He was very grumpy with Charlie, the man who gave him a bath once or twice a month. Once when Daddy heard him growling at Charlie, he stepped with Charlie into the bathroom next to the kitchen and gave Jerry a piece of his mind. Jerry never growled at Charlie again. He was undoubtedly a character. We had him for many, many years.

When mother played the piano, he slept under the piano, or tried to. After a while he couldn't stand it anymore, so he'd get up and walk out of the room. He felt that he should be there. He attempted to do what he thought was the polite thing to do. He was a noble little dog, and he was the dog I knew the best when I was very young.

I think we had a milkman whom Jerry would not let out of the truck. He drove up the long driveway and would be there wanting to bring the milk in, and Jerry didn't think that was suitable, and so he sat between him and the door until somebody came to get the milk. Beyond that I don't remember a great deal about him.

When I was a little older, Grandfather Herbert gave me a beautiful tri-color collie puppy that he got from his secretary. My grandfather called him Spike, so I did, too. Unfortunately, he did what collies sometimes do. They like to work. They like to be very busy. He met up with some neighborhood dogs and began to run with them. At our house, he liked to chase the chickens, but they were always safe inside their pen, and Spike was outside the fence, so unless somebody got out of the pen, no harm was done. Beyond our property lived dogs from other farms, and they liked to run sheep. Spike teamed up with them, and that was more exciting than chasing chickens he couldn't get to anyway. It's such a shame. He was so beautiful. The farmers wouldn't tolerate neighborhood dogs chasing their sheep, so one of them shot Spike. No one ever told me whether he had ever actually attacked a sheep, or went into the details about how he was shot, but one afternoon Spike didn't come home. That night my father told me that Spike had made some very unfortunate friends, and that his friends led him to a bad end. It was very sad.

One way or another, dogs teach us a great deal. Before my parents were married, my father had an Irish setter called Captain. They are so beautiful, but unfortunately because they are so beautiful, they are inbred quite a bit. So a lot of them are not very bright; they're flighty. A setter running is just so beautiful. They tend to have long hair on their tails, which can be brushed out into a beautiful plume. Daddy loved Cap. (He called him Cap for short.) Somehow, someone left a gate open, and he never saw Cap again. Cap had been his dog for five or six years at least. Daddy never got over it. In his eighties, he still remembered Captain and how much he loved him. He tried not to blame Cap's escape on anybody, but he feared that he knew who had left that gate open. He didn't want to hold it against that specific person because he might have been wrong, but Cap's loss always haunted him. I heard about Cap from the time I was very small.

We're a little crazy. We all have told secrets to our dogs, and they have probably heard more things than our contemporaries ever heard or knew. I've admitted things to my dog that I couldn't possibly tell my mother and father. I took lots of liberties telling my troubles to Donnie, who was the next dog in my life. He was a tenth-birthday present when we were living in Louisville. He always went to the country in the summer when we did, but when we came back to town, he came with us. That was a big sacrifice for my parents because we were in an apartment. He was an English springer spaniel, which is a little bit bigger than my dog here now, Murphy, a King Charles spaniel. He was a beautiful, sagacious hunting dog by trade, so to speak. He was smart, and he sensed when things were not happy for me. He spent a lot of time with my mother when I was at school. But when I came home, he was right there wherever I was.

I was responsible for Donnie all that summer. Because we were in town, we had to walk him. He taught me probably the lion's share of everything I learned about dogs. We made friends with people because anybody walking with a dog usually makes friends. He was a great learning lesson. No matter what was going on, I had to be sure he was fed right and that he got one egg a week in his food. Nothing could come before what I needed to do for Donnie. He was born at Christmas in a litter of seven puppies, all brown and white. All had big, gorgeous eyes. His brothers and sisters were named after Santa Claus's reindeer. Mine happened to be Donnie, or Donner. That's where the name came from. He had already been named by the kennel before I got him. In fact, the father of one of my school friends had the big kennel where Donnie was born, and he named the litter. He had the kennel and raised the puppies as a side interest, and he was very particular about the breeding of his dogs. He was very nice to let us have Donnie, though I'm sure he didn't give him to us; nonetheless,

Donnie had been my friend's puppy before he was given to me, and my friend told me his name.

Donnie brought enough ticks home that we had to fumigate the apartment. That was a joy! I thought my parents were awfully good to endure all that. The apartment was sealed up, and we went away for the weekend. We all lived through it. It was a good thing that my parents were still very young at that point. This was in mid- to late August. By that time Donnie was part of the family, so we had to go to a hotel for a while. That just tells you how crazy we all are about dogs. All is forgiven if you are a dog. It's okay.

I had Donnie until after I married. At first, Donnie came with me, after we came home from our honeymoon, when George and I moved into our little house on Belle Meade. But the routine was not what he was accustomed to. We realized that he would be happier with Mother and Daddy, whose house was further out. If they came to our house, they brought him too. He would visit, but he got back in the car with Mother and Daddy and went back home again. That was a better environment for him because our little house was just not far enough back from the road. I don't think he would have been out on the road on purpose, but he might have made a misjudgment.

Every morning Daddy would go to get the newspaper, and Donnie went with him. He never went on a leash. He walked all the way down the driveway by himself, found the paper, picked it up, and brought it back to Daddy. Then the two of them walked back to the house. It was just as regular as clockwork. Years later, one day it happened that, when Dad stepped off the porch to get the paper, Donnie didn't move a muscle. Daddy walked all the way down by himself and brought the paper back. Donnie walked into the house with him. Daddy said to Mother that morning, "You know, I think Donnie has retired." And he never went for the paper again. He lived another two years, at least. I know because I have pictures of Judy, our first daughter, with him. I think Cathy doesn't remember him, but she was the second one. He spent time with the girls and was a wonderful, wonderful friend. What a faithful and discreet friend he was to me! He heard all my secret thoughts, and he never blabbed.

About the time Judy was born, some friends gave George a beautiful German shepherd, a female. Her name was Josephine. Her papers indicated that she was related to Rin Tin Tin. She looked the part. She just lay around and kept watch. Like Jerry, she didn't let the milkman out of the truck either. I think he was too noisy. She would go to the door and stand between the kitchen and the milkman's truck. We had an on-again, off-again housekeeper who would go out and get the milk. Jo never growled at anybody. When the baby came, she would get up from where she had chosen to sleep and come and lie right against my upper leg while I would sit and feed and rock the baby at night. When I would stand up to go tuck her back in, Jo would go back to her place. She always sat, lay really, just lay down right against my feet and kept them warm. She was so sweet and so gentle.

I always felt that she was telling me things. "Don't forget to do the so and so." I loved her dearly.

I would push Judy in her stroller, and Josephine would join us as we walked up and down Belle Meade Boulevard and the adjoining streets. She didn't run off or suddenly go back home. She always did what a well-trained German shepherd would do. As we were coming home one afternoon, there was, of course, the Belle Meade bus. We stopped because they stopped, wanting to be sure they saw us. We walked across in front of the bus and Jo was just a little ahead of me, and somebody came down Belle Meade, swerved around that stopped bus and hit Jo. It didn't kill her, but she was badly injured. The bus driver got off and pitched a fit. It was amazing; that man was so mad. Of course, we didn't have telephones in the car then, but the bus driver told some people gathered around, "Get a policeman. I'm stopping this car right now. We're arresting these people."

In the meantime, of course, we had to get help for Jo. That man in the car came pretty fast around the bus and knocked her over into the green median area. She didn't survive. That's why we didn't have Jo nearly as long as we would have wanted. That was the first German shepherd we ever had.

We got our second one when we moved to Louisville. We moved because George was building a large subdivision there. Judy was almost two, and Cathy had just been born. We had one of the little houses George was building. One day he came home with a German shepherd that we named Baron. He was bigger than Jo had been, but he was big even for a German shepherd. There were a lot of workmen on the place doing all kinds of labor, and George just thought it would be a good idea if it was known that we had this big dog. He also took me out one afternoon and showed me how to use his shotgun, because, he said, I might need it one day.

Baron was a wonderful dog, but he wasn't much help one time when I could have used a great watchdog. George had left me with the two baby girls and Baron while he went on a business trip. That night, I heard some men on the front porch, and the shadows I saw on the window shades in a room on the side of the house made me very nervous. I couldn't think what those men were up to, but I knew it couldn't be good, so I got George's shotgun out and loaded it up. After thinking about whether I should say anything, I said loudly to whoever was out there, "I don't intend to have you on my porch!" They thought that was funny, so I decided to give them something else to laugh about. In the firmest voice I could muster, I said, "I have my husband's shotgun, and I know how to shoot it!" I could hear that my toughest voice came out all wobbly, but I pointed the shotgun right at the front door and said, "I really am going to pull the trigger!" And I did. The gun roared, spewed out smoke and flame, slammed my shoulder, and fired its lead right through the door. We didn't find any bodies on the porch, but those men didn't give me any more trouble. Though I couldn't believe I had actually pulled the trigger, the holes in the front door proved what I had done. Meanwhile, I had no idea where Baron was. He must have been somewhere else in the house, fast asleep.

He stayed with us for the almost three years that we lived in Louisville. George was home in Nashville one weekend and bought the fifty-two acre Old Hickory property. In the meantime, Baron was as faithful and as smart and as low-key and as gentle with the children as you could have dreamed a dog could be. He was more silver than Jo had been. He was well marked and very, very handsome, and sagacious, a great comfort to me and all the children. When Cathy was learning to crawl and would totter, he would go and help keep her from falling if he could. He paid awfully good attention to her, as if she were his little puppy. He felt responsible to be sure she was all right. By that time Judy was walking very well and he didn't seem to feel that he had to pay as much attention to her as he did to Cathy, this puppy, this little one.

We had him until we moved back to Nashville, and we'd been here for about a year and a half or two years, I think, at least. He had distemper. That's pneumonia for a dog, basically. I remember getting up and sleeping in the breakfast room with him. I'm not sure why. It wasn't that he was having trouble breathing, but he was very sick. We just didn't go to bed and leave him by himself. We needed to have him sleep in the house where we could take good care of him. We did this for quite a while, and he recovered. He developed something that was a complication from the distemper. We nursed him all the way through it and thought, "Oh, we've made it." Then a few months later he became ill and died soon afterwards. He didn't recover as well as we thought he had.

We had two other German shepherds. Judy was in the first class of women students at the University of the South. She bought a puppy from a cardboard box that was in front of the Supply Store. These puppies belonged to the Sewanee chief of police. Judy had scraped up thirty or forty dollars and bought that puppy. She had to keep him in her dormitory, which was against the rules, until she was able to come home. She smuggled him here, there, and yonder. His name was Eli. There is a painting of him downstairs in the living room. Eli was a mountain dog. He liked to carry rocks. You could throw a rock and he'd run get it and bring it back. You could teach him to get a stick, but somehow, we think, because he was born in the mountains, he liked rocks better. He also took boards, if he could find a loose board on a fence. We had a lot of fences because of the horses, and he would get a loose board off the fence and walk around balancing this board. It was unbelievable how he could do it. Every now and again he tried to walk between trees and he couldn't get through, so we teased him.

He was a dear, sweet dog. He meant the world to everybody and took good care of the children. Occasionally, he broke down and chased a horse, which you have to take exception to. In the first place, he'd get his head kicked off. Basically he had to learn to stay away from the horses' feet. He loved the new foals. When they came, he went down and spent time with them at the barn. When they were out in the fields, that was different. He learned to steer clear of them. He grew up across the road from where we live now. We kept Eli forever. He was named for Judy's best beau, Eric Luther Ison (E-L-I), a young man from California who would become her husband and Jennifer's father.

Eli had work to do, or so he thought. He did guard duty and lay on the front yard and watched anything that came through the front gate. He began to have trouble with his hips, so this made it harder for him to do his job, but he stayed at is as long as he could.

George got another German shepherd. His silver eyebrows were very prominent against his dark face, so he was called Bismarck, or Mark for short. Mark took over, and it was clear. At first, Eli taught him what he wanted him to do. We watched him lie out there in the yard with Eli. He would get up to wander off, and Eli would apparently fuss at him. Mark would come back and lie down again. Then, little by little, he began to go down by the gate and run beside a car coming up the driveway. Eli was way down in the back, which was sad. German shepherds have a tendency to have hip trouble. Eventually, so did Mark, but much, much later. We gave both dogs everything that the veterinarian could think of to help them.

We had some other dogs, but we always had to have at least one German shepherd, and Mark was with us the longest. Both he and Eli went with the girls as they went riding down Old Hickory Boulevard for a Pony Club lesson or event, or just for a ride in the park. First Eli started out, and then Mark picked this up when Eli no longer could.

Sallie's cat Evil deserves special mention. I never had much use for Evil because learned to hide behind any door and jump out and grab your legs and sink his claws into your calves. Sallie said, "I hate to tell you, but I taught him how to do that." Do you wonder how he got his name?

Oliver was a little gray poodle that Susan and Robin found advertised in the paper when they were quite young. He was with us for around fifteen years, and it seemed as though he might live forever. When Susan was in the hospital with a rather serious condition, Oliver went down to the barn and met a tragic death when he encountered a pack of dogs that sometimes roamed. I sure hated going back to the hospital and telling Susan about Oliver.

Murphy is my Cavalier King Charles spaniel. He likes to sit with me most of the time, and we get along very well. Annie was Murphy's predecessor, the first Cavalier King Charles spaniel that I had. She was a gift from Judy after George died, and I had her for quite a long time. Cavaliers are good companions in the house. In the field, they are good bird-hunting dogs.

One time, when Susan's son John was small, he took Annie out for a walk. After a little while, he came back and rang the doorbell. At the door I found a long-faced little boy with Annie on the leash. John said, "Grandmother, I have bad news again."

I said, "What's the problem? Are you all right?"

He said, "Yes, ma'am. But Annie and I were walking, and all of a sudden, some birds flew up, and Annie jumped in the air and caught one. And she ate it!"

I said, "Well, I am sorry about that, but it wasn't your fault. You couldn't help it. These dogs are hunting dogs, and that's built into their system. You just plain love popcorn, and she just plain loves anything that flies. So don't feel bad about it."

We had a pair of Japanese Chins, black and white sisters, very small dogs. One of them belonged to Susan, who lived pretty much across the road. Her dog was Daphne, and mine was Hyacinth. They each knew where the other one lived, and quite often they would sneak off and go back and forth, paying each other visits across the street. I'd never had little dogs like that before, and we enjoyed them both. Daphne was over visiting in our garden, but then we didn't see her for a little bit. We found her later. She'd had a heart attack and died under a bush in the garden.

When her sister Hyacinth was still young, she started showing signs of not being well. Actually, the vet said that she wasn't going to get well. She sat in my lap while he gave her the shot to end her suffering. She stayed with me until she didn't care anymore. That was sad for all of us. Everybody loved those two little dogs. It turned out that those sisters were from a litter of five girls, and every last one of them died of a heart problem within a short time of each other. Daphne was the first one to go, and she was probably not more than three. Hyacinth lived a little bit longer.

Muldoon is the one that really makes me laugh. If you think of an English bulldog named Muldoon, now you know he is behind the bar somewhere. He belonged to Robin's son Gus when he was little.

Horses, Revisited

I can't believe Old Hickory Boulevard was a place where you could go out our gate and ride your horse over to the park. I wouldn't think of having anybody do it now. But it was quieter then. Our children rode over to the park where the golf course is. Back then it was just open pasture.

Once they had reached a certain level, they could go to the park in pairs, but we preferred groups of three. No one was allowed to go alone. They would go through the park where you see the golf course now and all the way up into the hills. They knew the area extremely well. They would ride a little bit further into the park for their Pony Club meetings. So we might send as many as three or four or five children, when Robin got to where she would join them. When Robin was four, she was really pretty able on the appropriate pony. They all looked after each other. They still shake their heads when we remember what they used to do without thinking twice about it, not believing that they were able to do it then.

Mark, our German shepherd, went with them quite often. Every now and again they would think that he had gone too far, and yell at him, and send him home. That didn't always work. Mark would go off and hide for a while, and they'd go on to the meeting. Then he'd show up at the Pony Club meeting. It was such a free, happy existence.

George however did not ride unless there was a picnic at the other end of it. He was more interested in what he was doing at school. He would ride with them in the park, but the girls were interested in riding with the proper everything. Hands needed to be right, heels needed to be right. They were taught that way from the beginning at the Pony Club. It was second nature to them.

Once, when my granddaughter in Columbia, South Carolina, was seven or eight, I asked her mother, "Now, what's Julia Claire going to want for

Christmas?" I'd find out several things. I was remembering when my daughter Julia and her sisters were about that age, they wanted things like a new nose band or a new girth for Christmas. They always wanted some piece of riding tack, something for the shows coming up.

They had to keep everything leather in perfect shape, in show-worthy condition. I remember seeing them sitting on the kitchen floor with the pieces of leather they were working on all over the floor. They all learned how to put all those many pieces back together. I never could have done it. That was the kind of thing that was important to them then.

Training for Life

Robin, Sallie, and Judy are still riding, though they no longer do the jumping and so on that they used to compete in. Sallie also did a lot of dressage. Whatever facet of their riding they were particularly attuned to, they really loved it. It was the best training in the world. They knew that when they came home from a show, even though they wanted a bath more than anything, they first had a litany of things that had to be done, including cleaning their ponies' feet, watering, brushing, and cooling out; whatever their ponies needed, it all had to be done before they could get themselves to the house and head for the bathtub. They had to take care of their ponies before they took care of themselves.

I wouldn't take anything in the world for the training this experience gives. I think that's the reason my daughters are and have been good mothers as they've come along. I couldn't have put nearly as much emphasis as the Pony Club did on what you need to do in what order. Parents couldn't have done anything like as well as the Pony Club did. I'm very grateful for that background. I wouldn't have had the wisdom to get across to them, and I would have talked too much.

They learned with other people, their peers, so that they were striving to do what everybody else was doing, and learning lessons indirectly, instead of having their parents teach them that directly. It was an effective way of getting them to want to learn what they needed for life. Now their Pony Club training is ingrained in the way they do everything. I noticed that when Susan was having to organize the gathering for her son and his fiancée this past weekend. As someone very active in work and in matters away from home, she's not particularly a homebody, but she can put things in proper order. I will sometimes ask, "Have you thought about so and so? What do you want to do about that?"

She will say, "No, I can't get to that yet. I'm thinking about it, and I haven't made any decisions about that now. I will take care of it later, after I do this first."

She's thinking in order. I see it in Cathy always. Though she wasn't a big a Pony Clubber, she still did it all.

While we were building the house at 2228 Old Hickory, we moved into a little house on River Road, west of Nashville. George had bought it without my having a chance to see it. I suppose he thought it would be fine until we could move into the nice house he was building us, and we really were. But when he first came home with the news that he had bought a house on River Road, I naturally had some questions about the rooms and layout. He drew me up the floor plan to the best of his recollection. I studied it this way and that, but I thought there must be something wrong with the plan he had drawn. I asked, "Does it have a bathroom?" He had to think about that one for a while. At first he was pretty sure it didn't have a tub or a shower, but he thought it must have a toilet; he just didn't recall seeing one. When we moved into the house, we learned that our neighbors across the street lived in a bus. They owned several pet turkeys that always came out front to watch our ponies.

What our little house lacked on the inside, it made up for in the barn that came with the house. A pony named Flowers came with the barn. While we all came to love Flowers, she was not all joy to live with. Flowers's goal in life, it seemed, was to step on my feet. Truly, if she saw me nearby, she'd move over and put her foot on mine. I can't think of why she would have done a thing like that. But Judy had a wonderful experience with Flowers.

Judy would get up each morning and go out to see Flowers. Judy was maybe five and a half. One morning, after her customary visit to Flowers in the barn, she came in the house and said something about Flowers's baby. Because she went out to say good morning to Flowers, she had witnessed the birth of this new baby pony. We knew she was going to have a baby, but we had no idea when, because the people we got her from didn't tell us anything about her.

Lo and behold, when we arrived at the barn to see what had happened, it was just as Judy had said. By this time, Baby was standing up fairly well. Fortunately, Flowers had a big enough stall so she had lots of room.

Judy just happened upon a pony having a baby horse. That's how the lesson was taught. It didn't surprise or upset her, but it could have terrified her. She just said, "Here's the baby." Many such things have happened to us, and I have been grateful for them but take no credit for any of them. Since then, we've had a number of brood mares, and they've been taken to

Lexington to be bred. Many baby ponies and horses were born, and sweet old Flowers was our best teacher.

Although my son George was never particularly interested in the horses, when we had a new baby coming, George started paying attention. When the mother was not able to feed her baby adequately, George helped me make big buckets of baby formula, and together we would carry them down to the barn to feed the baby ponies. He saw ponies from little bitty, and as a young boy and teenager, he loved them brand new. When my husband George was out of town, or if the girls were at school or not at home, he'd go down to the barn with me to help me feed. So he learned much from living with horses, too, though in a way different from the girls. It's a great thing to be in the country. Our children grew up close to a reality that most people don't care too much about, but our children appreciated the experience they had.

Jaunuary 11, 2016

CHAPTER IX
A Life of Faith

Early Experiences of Church

Throughout my childhood, I attended the Episcopal Church with my family. There were so many things I loved about my childhood religious upbringing, and I still have warm and happy memories of those years. One of my earliest memories is of a neighbor in Louisville. We lived in an apartment in town at 1041 Cherokee Road in the winter, because the countryside in Kentucky is sometimes rough in the coldest months. I went to school in town. In the apartment next to us was a girl named Barbara, and I don't even know for sure what her last name was. She was about a year older than I. She was Catholic, and I believe she attended Sacred Heart Academy. She wore a uniform, as did I in my school. We sat on the front porches of our respective apartments when the weather allowed. She helped me walk my dog Donnie, so we talked a lot.

I was mostly impressed by the books she had that were based on her religion. She was reading a book to prepare her for her first communion. I was fascinated by the pictures. I remember pictures of little girls in white dresses, veils, and flowers. The book described what she would be experiencing when she took communion. She would tell me what she was getting ready to do. That big day approached, and we were so excited together.

She had me come over and see her dress and veil. What little girl doesn't love to go look at a dress and veil? I admired the embroidery that was on the veil. We shared the joy of getting ready for something very special. I knew from her books what her first communion was going to be like. The girls in their white dresses and veils would be part of a procession with the acolytes and the priest. They would kneel during the Mass, and they would look up at the altar. There was just a lot of beauty and I remember being very impressed with it.

She was learning prayers and responses. The priest and the bishop would be there. It all becomes quite real to me again: the pleasure, the joy, and the anticipation. All of that took form in a little girl's mind. And then she told me about it afterwards, and described what some of her friends were feeling. After it was over, she brought me some little mementos from her first communion.

Then a few years later, I remember my own confirmation at St. James' Church in Pewee Valley, where we lived in the summer. I was confirmed at nine years old, a younger age than was normal, but that's when the bishop could get there. The bishop came on my birthday, as it happened, May 19, and that made it terribly personal. There were only three of us in my little parish who were confirmed, one other girl and a boy. This was also our first communion.

I felt warmth and love for the church, as I felt warmly loved by the church. Father Board, the vicar of St. James', lived in a little house right next to the church, and his mother kept house for him and made us cookies. The whole environment was wonderful as I remember it. There were lots of things to learn, and all the things we talked about were interesting. We met for the confirmation class in the back of the church. So we learned right there, and we walked up to the front of the church and went to the altar where we were shown the chalice, the paten, the cruets, the altar book, and the linens. We learned about what was used in the church services and the colors of the seasons. The three of us were allowed to help change the altar hangings to the appropriate color as the seasons changed.

I'd love to know something about what it was like for the other two that went through that confirmation class with me. After I was about thirteen or fourteen, I lost track of them. We moved, and they moved.

I remember being very impressed when I watched Mother, who worked with the altar society at St. James', as she ironed the linens and put them in tissue paper to take them back to church. She did her altar society work with such care and reverence. We were very integrated into the church because it was small. It was important to all of us, and each member was very important to the church.

When my children were brought up in the Catholic Church, they learned the Catechism by rote. We didn't do much memory work, other than the Lord's Prayer and the Apostles' Creed and other things we memorized without knowing we were learning them, just because we used them in church so much. Our classes emphasized learning concepts, and we were encouraged to comment on some of the basic stories of the Bible and try to work out for ourselves what they meant. I loved the Sermon on the Mount as a child. Our experience was nothing like the way some Baptist children learned Bible verses by chapter and verse.

We learned the miracle of the loaves and the fishes and other miracle stories and some of the parables. The story of Jesus healing the man born blind meant a lot to me. I was impressed that, though he was blind, he did not grovel, but had strong confidence in himself. After he was healed, he understood that Jesus must have been at least a good man rather than a man who had no respect for God or the law.

I had a hard time figuring out who the Pharisees were because I'd never encountered any people like that—people you needed to stand up to because of the way they were, who used religion to take advantage of other people. As I grew older, I learned to understand more of the political situation at the time and the tension between the Jews and the Romans, as well as between Jesus and the Pharisees. We knew that there were bad people and better people.

Father Board was pretty good about feeling us out and seeing which of the three of us were beginning to understand. I generally talk too much, so if I didn't get it, he knew it. I loved those sessions in the back of the church, as our so-called catechism was going along. Father Board, I learned later, lived to be in his nineties. I think his first name was Robert, but I may not be right about that. I had real affection for him because he had lots of patience, and if we had questions, he would try his best to help us get it. One of the three of us was going through the class but wasn't really interested. The boy and I asked a good many questions and talked more in detail. Father Board talked to all three of us, but the other girl didn't seem very interested to me. That must have been frustrating for him because even I understood that she was there only because her parents brought her. That seemed to be as far as it went. But the other two of us, I think we enjoyed the class and looked forward to it. It was easy to like the hot chocolate and cookies that Mrs.

Board always brought us. She also contributed to creating the warm, safe environment that I loved.

We moved to Pittsburgh in the late summer of 1941, before the United States got involved in World War II. My mother and I went to Trinity Cathedral there, and Father joined us when he was free. I remember being very impressed with it because, particularly after St. James', it was grand and glorious on a completely different scale. The music took my breath away. Because of the wonderful choirmaster, just going to that church educated me in church music. After being used to very simple music at St. James', I was overwhelmed. When we went to church in Pittsburgh, we would walk into this huge cathedral and hear a choir that was so well-trained it was almost miraculous. I'm moved and amazed that human beings can create such music that it gives you the chills. Episcopal Church music, if it can be lumped together this way, is impressive. The cathedral had a marvelous organ and a fine organist, and I do not, to this day, particularly like organ music except when it's well done. They had concerts that my mother took me to quite often. She was educated to appreciate music because of her mother. These concerts were part of the whole church routine all through the year, and particularly at Easter. That was a big transition from our little church that I loved. I'm loving it to this day, along with processions and all the beauty and elegance that went with being there. You just wanted to drop to your knees.

Going to the cathedral made Sundays into uniquely glorious days in a period that, for me and my parents, was not a joyous one. I didn't love living in Pittsburgh at all, but Sundays were different. You almost couldn't get out of bed and get into the slush and the snow and the cold without thinking, "I've got to make it." I really wanted to be there on my knees, and that has always stayed with me. I was only in Pittsburgh for about one year, but going to the cathedral was what helped me get through. I was twelve when we moved, and the next few years were a difficult age, and you don't know who you are when you are taken out of the environment where you grew up. I think so much of children of military people who are moved from place to place during their childhood, when they are learning so much and growing up in so many ways. You need some kind of an anchor to help you grow emotionally and understand things that are changing around you. I found that anchor in my family and in my church.

Childhood and Youth during World War II

During these years, my father was the assistant treasurer for Alcoa Aluminum. He was travelling some, but he was usually home on weekends. At night, he was often away at meetings and on projects for Alcoa. That was a terribly busy time during the war. Daddy was very involved because Alcoa was a large company, and they made many products that were used for the war. They would say, "Alcoa is involved in helping the war," but details weren't given, and we didn't ask for them much either. Pittsburgh was such an important manufacturing center that it would have been an excellent target for the Germans to attack, so we did have blackouts, times when we had to turn off all the lights at night to prepare for bombing attacks. I truly had the sense that America was in a fight between good and evil, and that we were on the side of the good, and that my father was helping.

Hitler was such an example of evil that there was no debating it. We knew English children were being sent out of London and some of the main cities to the countryside. We each knew, or thought we knew, what it would have felt like if our parents had to send us to the country, and if we were being bombed. We had blackouts at night, so we were thinking that we could be bombed. It never happened, thank God, but nonetheless, when you pull all the curtains, and don't have any light glowing, there is a certain suspense as you wait for what might happen.

Daddy was an air raid warden, on top of everything else he did. Donnie would sit on the cedar chest in front of the big windows that were closed down and howl while the air raid warnings were going off. I remember sitting with him, telling him, "Don't worry. It's going to be all right." The alarm was frightening at first, but Donnie's howling made the situation slightly comical.

We were all very Anglicized at that point; at least everybody I knew was. We had emotional ups and downs. This was the only time I ever remember being particularly affected by what went on beyond my own environment. We were aware of what was happening in the war in different parts of the world. Of course, if you went to the movies at all, you saw the newsreels in the movie theaters. They were all black and white, very dramatic, with narration given by a man with exactly the right voice to convey a serious sense of urgency. We saw soldiers, airplanes, and ships in the newsreels. I was growing up in a world at war, and I knew it as a child.

Since we didn't have television then, the movie theater was the only place where we saw film of what was happening. We studied geography a lot in those years, so we knew where Germany, France, England, Russia, and Japan were and what they looked like on the map, and how wide the English Channel was. I remember having to write in where the city of Berlin was on the map of

Germany. We knew how close these countries were to each other. We knew all this off the top of our heads.

I learned all these things by the time I was twelve or thirteen, so I have trouble understanding why sometimes children today don't know where things are. They will show you a little bit of something on television, saying that something went from one place to another. But to connect names with places and to know where events are happening in the world is something that doesn't seem so important to people now. It seems to me it should be more important. It certainly was for us. Knowing these things helped us feel involved. We knew where troop movements were and what was happening, particularly when Germany began to fall apart. It was very real to us as children.

As for what was happening to the Jews in Germany and the lands taken by Hitler, we did not know in detail what we know now, but we knew about *Kristallnacht*. I remember hearing that over the news broadcast at night and not quite getting it, and yet understanding that it was disastrous, and it was wicked, and it was not in any way, shape, or form, an acceptable thing to do to people. *Kristallnacht* told us what Germany was about. We were also aware of what was happening to Poland, which was light blue on my map. It was emphasized more later. I can't separate now quite as well as to what we did know and understand at the time. I know that at Winchester Thurston, they didn't talk to us a lot about what was happening, other than all the map work we had to do.

We knew about the bombing of London in detail. We knew how brave the King and Queen of England were to stay in London. Sometimes we knew somebody who had been there during some bombing and came back to the States. There was an awful lot of connection between the two countries.

A Decision for Family Unity

I did not decide to become a Roman Catholic until George and I had been married about a year. When George and I began to date, I had already been exposed to the Catholic Church since about first grade. George had gone to the youth group with me at Christ Episcopal Church in downtown Nashville. I was surprised at how willing he was to go with me, and to sit on the floor and listen to Peyton Williams, the priest at Christ Church, talk about the Episcopal Church and what it means to be a member of the Church. It was obvious that the Church was very important to George. The more I knew him, the more I knew how much his growing up in the church had colored who he was and the way he dealt with people and how scrupulously honest he was. We've walked out of a restaurant when he's realized he had too much change, and he would go back and return the money. Little things like that showed who he was.

At the same time, he knew a little about me, too, so he said he would like to meet Mr. Williams, who was a little watchful of me because he realized I was serious about George and his church. So he was nice enough to invite us to meet with him, and George was nice enough to go. That's how we began to sit down and get to know each other better and eat popcorn and learn. I didn't see any point in bringing it up with my parents at that point.

I don't think George ever expected me to join the Catholic Church. He knew our church was important to me and to my family. At the same time, I was watching him. I knew more and more that his faith was a very big part of who he was—a part to which I was particularly attracted.

Time went on. After we married, we moved to Louisville and lived there three years, at the end of which I had definitely decided that I was going to join the Catholic Church. In the meantime, I took instruction with Father Greenwell at St. Raphael's Church in Louisville. I went one afternoon a week to sit and talk with him.

I would ask George to drop me off there. I just said I had volunteered to do something with the children's department. I didn't tell him I was talking to Father Greenwell.

I didn't say a word to him about it until I had made up my mind, after I had been going about three or four months and really was doing something with the children's department as well. I didn't want to put any pressure on him at all. I knew he wouldn't want to put any on me. Although on Easter and on other special occasions, George took me to Grace Episcopal Church, which was fairly close to us. Sometimes he stayed with the children so I could go. We went to the Catholic Church every other Sunday morning, so it must have been a little obvious where this was going. But I think it's very important to go to church together. Finally I told him, "I think I'm going to join the Catholic Church."

He resisted, saying, "Be careful. I don't want you to do that." He was extremely reluctant to have me do it for a while, because he thought I was doing it for him. I was not doing it for him, but I was doing it because of him, because of who he was, and I knew what guided what he did.

During this time, which was around 1955, I was praying that the impediments to both churches would appear in a realistic and not overdramatized way. Both were having problems with different issues at the time. The churches actually were speaking to one another some during this time. I was drawn to both. I prayed that the differences would be clarified.

Everybody who learns anything about the Episcopal Church and the Roman Catholic Church learns about Henry VIII, Philip II of Spain, and

Elizabeth I and the Spanish Armada. So much history goes with both churches. In 1955, some priests were leaving the Catholic Church over the issue of marriage, and some Episcopal priests were joining the Catholic Church because they became convinced it was the only church for them. You could read articles all over the place about issues relating to both churches and the times we were in. There were rumblings here, there, and yonder.

I didn't see why George and I couldn't kneel together in prayer and let this settle, if it would. Both churches are full of good people, and they all want the same things, basically. We found in talking to Episcopal and Catholic clergy no great reasons why both churches couldn't kneel together and become one. They may never be one in our lifetime, but both churches are good at heart, and they're letting an awful lot of real trivia, which they don't see as trivia, get in the way. The simple truth is that everybody is asking the same things of heaven, and we all want to grant one another and everyone else peace. All of the other things that they bring up and debate over are far removed from the simple purpose of the Church, which is to be one with God.

Nothing I believed in or was taught in the Episcopal Church was negated, but when I joined the Roman Catholic Church, I wanted to be part of a church that I admired because of what it meant to my husband, and I wanted us to go to church together and to raise our family in the same church.

I knew my decision would cause my parents to suffer, and it did. That may be why I am so hesitant in speaking about leaving the Episcopal Church and joining the Catholic Church. My mother was very distressed at first and was very sorry. I still regret the pain my leaving the Episcopal Church caused her. She was crazy about George, but what church you belong to is a matter of your beliefs, what you believe to be true about God and creation and how we are supposed to live. You either believe the faith or you do not; you don't just change churches for convenience. I didn't know how to make this decision any easier for my parents other than for us to live as smoothly and peacefully as we could. All we could do was try to prove that we were fine. My mother eventually got used to my decision.

Daddy got used to George. He grew very fond of George. He certainly didn't expect to! He did get a little upset when the sixth child came along, but when we named her Robin, after him (Robert Read), it was some small consolation for the fact that we had so many children.

The Importance of Clean Socks

When it came to bringing up our children in the Church, that went well and smoothly. I was concerned about matters like getting the children dressed. I would get up in the morning and say, "It's Sunday. Put on clean socks, please." When we picked up Grandmother Hicks to bring her with us, she would check their socks. When you are taking six children to church, inevitably somebody has got on a dirty sock. There are no two ways about it. She was very stiff-necked about clothes. She looked at everybody right and left. Socks were a big problem. That's the way families are. But we knew where we would be on any Sunday morning, and we all went together.

Grandmother Hicks (George's mother) never seemed too grateful that I had joined her church. It was what she expected. There wasn't going to be any choice about it. It took a long time for her to forgive me for not being Alice Tyne. In all my life, I had never met anybody like Mother Hicks.

She wasn't German for nothing. She grew up in the church right next door to her family's home in Louisville. There's a definite side of Louisville that is heavily German Catholic. It's definitely different and it's not Nashville Catholic either. When a different understanding of something is deeply bred into a person, it takes a long time to shake that. I'd never met anybody like her, and she had never intended to meet anyone like me.

So Mom (what our family always called Grandmother Hicks) always referred to Judy, the one who was not named for her, whom George had named for my grandmother Julia, as that little "rug rat," which didn't make me happy. I knew better than to say, "I really wish you wouldn't say that," because that would not have worked. Little by little, time went on, and one thing led to another, and after several years she moved in and lived with us until the day she died in our house.

Mom taught the four youngest children to play a game called "Stealing Casino," and also, as it turned out, how to cheat! The children used to play other card games with her in shifts because none of them had the stamina to keep up with her one on one. I think they won her over, particularly Robin, who was about four when Mom came to live with us. She used to play cards with Robin in the library, and they both cheated outrageously. It was just terrible. Robin also learned to play chess very young, though not with Mom, who didn't play chess. I only mention that because Robin was just kind of canny.

Julia was born in 1951. Robin was born in 1961. I think we had six in twelve years. So Grandmother Hicks happened to come to live with us in

1968. She had an apartment on West End, where she moved after they sold the house across the street that she had had for many years. We used to pick her up every Sunday morning and take her to church because she didn't drive. Then we'd bring her out to our house to have lunch.

One Sunday, she was holding her shoulder funny, so we asked what had happened. It turned out, she hated to tell us, she had slipped on the driveway that went up to her apartment and had fallen. She must have hurt her shoulder, we thought.

"Let's take a look at that. Have you been to the...?"

"No," she said.

Anyway, she had broken her arm and was such a soldier that she wasn't going to tell anybody. We, of course, took her to the hospital as soon as we found out. She was incapacitated for a while, so we brought her out to stay with us for a week or two while that got better. She hated being with us because our house was out here on Old Hickory Boulevard. She felt like she was way out in the country and couldn't go out and get on the bus and do what she wanted to do. George took her back and forth to where she needed to go. Her arm finally healed, and she was glad to get back in her apartment. He picked her up every Thursday for lunch and to take her to the grocery, and we still continued to pick her up Sunday morning. Little by little, we could see that she wasn't really quite herself.

I never knew exactly how old she was, ever. And there was a debate between George's brother Charles and his sister Mary about which of them was older. I really never knew. I think the brother was the older one, but Mary wanted to be the older one. They were always at each other about who came first.

George's father became a Catholic because he joined his wife's church. Once he did that, the people in Mississippi never again bothered him about preaching. Eventually he became Grand Knight of the Knights of Columbus, the equivalent of president. So it was because of Grandmother Hicks that our family became Catholic.

Grandmother Hicks

I didn't think I'd ever say this, but I can almost say I grew to love her, because she was gutsy. She was extremely admirable, but she was not normally reasonable. It must have been just awful for her to have to end up living in our house. Having her live with us was good for all of the children. They learned how to adjust to her because she was herself, always; but no matter how disagreeable she was every now and again, they learned to see the funny side of what she did.

Young George had a wry sense of humor about his grandmother at a very early age. When he was seven or eight, one day he came into the kitchen and said, "I've just gone by Grandmother Hicks' room, and she is doing her jaybird act."

I left the room and went through the dining room and into the living room and laughed, but George knew I thought this was funny, or he wouldn't have said anything to me. I thought, "That's cool; that's very cool." There was a large window in his grandmother's room, and a wing chair. When she would get out of the tub, she liked to sit in front of that window, and sometimes she didn't trouble herself about putting on clothes first. She never knew George would see her doing this enough to call it her "jaybird act," and I am so glad she didn't. I'm glad he didn't step in and say hello.

She, too, had to learn to adjust, but the children didn't quite see it that way. She had to put up with living there in a house full of six children. This was totally different from anything she'd ever done. She also had to put up with somebody else making the grocery list and doing things she would normally have wanted to do herself. She was used to being in charge. When she could no longer live on her own, she had to give up an awful lot of freedom and power.

Her daughter Mary only came to see her at our house one time. She was so mad that we had Mom with us, but she couldn't have lived with Mary. Mary's second story of an apartment out by Warner Park had no elevator. Mom could not have walked up those steps at all. It was a small apartment anyway. Mary was in real estate, and she came and went quite a bit. At Mary's there was nobody who could take care of Mom.

She had one or two friends who lived a good distance away, and she rarely saw them. I thought she must miss them, so one day I said, "Don't you want to have some ladies for lunch?" Two or three of them lived on Hillsboro Road. They went way back, though I don't know that there was much of a friendship, but it was good enough. "Wouldn't you like to have Mrs...?" She seemed not to want to very badly, but she decided to do it, anyway.

We set up for the lunch in the dining room, which was no big deal because we ate in the dining room every night. We took one leaf out of the table so it didn't look too long. I took two or three different things to her, saying, "Would you like to use this china or would you like to use this?" and "Let's plan the menu." We did and she was a little bit excited about it, actually. It was sort of beyond her to let anybody else know. There were just four ladies coming. I said to her, "I'm really sorry, I didn't realize it at the time"—which was a tale—"but I'm going to have to be at the school to help with something, so I won't be here." I made that up. "Don't you want to sit at the head of the table?" We set it up so that she could run the whole show, except Maddie, who helped in the kitchen, was grumbling a little bit.

"You aren't going to be here?" Maddie asked.

I replied, "No."

When the guests arrived, I greeted them at the door and led the ladies in. I had Mom in the living room. She could run her own show. There was a little bell that she could ring, and Maddie would know that she was ready for her to bring in the lunch. I thought she needed me gone. That was the only way I could figure it out. Louise Linton, who lived next door around the corner, picked me up, and we went to the drugstore and had lunch. I think it went pretty well, but Mom was a little nervous when I left. When I got back, I think she thought she had a good time.

That lunch is the only thing I can remember doing for her that I think was probably a pretty good thing. I think she appreciated it in her own way. It was good that I had gotten out of her hair. After all, she had run a house for a long, long time, and it must have been very hard to be living where somebody else was in charge, and it wasn't anybody she liked very much anyway.

I recognize that it was very hard for Mom not to be running things. She was a pretty courageous girl, really, in a lot of ways. She had married George's father and they had moved to Mississippi. Before that, she had lived next door to her Catholic church in Louisville. Talk about a different environment! She adjusted and she had two children there, too. Her husband had died suddenly when young, and her younger son had gone off to fight in World War II. It took me a while to appreciate what her whole experience had been. She had grown up in a family of five girls and four boys, too, I think. Maybe some of them were cousins, but they were all very close. Then she had to put up with me and with George not doing what she had in mind that he would do, because I was not Alice Tyne and never would be. She was half-mad at him for quite a while, I think. It wasn't easy being Mom.

I do think she eventually almost got attached to me, though. She began to ask, when she was less well, what I thought about certain things. She would ask if I thought she was supposed to take the medicine before or after meals. This was nothing really, but it was a deferring to my opinion, and that was very, very hard for her. When she needed to ask for help, she began to trust me more.

New Nightgowns

We thought Mom needed some new nightgowns, so we bought some. She liked them fairly well, but there was an old white flannel nightgown that she felt warm in. All these others were flannel too, because she liked that texture. Mom pretty much stayed in her room, and I began to realize that she was not doing very well. She had a heart condition that was gradually getting worse.

We got somebody who could sit up with her at night, a young black woman who was really cute. She came every evening about 7:30 or 8:00 p.m. She would take over and sit in Mom's room all night. With Mom in her white nightgown and tucked in bed, they'd listen to the radio until she went to sleep. I am so indebted to this night nurse. I don't remember her name. She was as little as she could be, tiny. She was so excited because she was engaged to be married. She brought a box one evening to show me a beautiful, very fluffy, red nightgown. She wanted to show it to somebody and I was flattered to no end that she would let me in on her private life. We, of course, tried to get something to go with it. She was sweet to have included me in the excitement. She reminded me of Butterfly McQueen, who was in *Gone With the Wind*, the little girl with the little bitty voice. She stayed nights with Mom for about three weeks, or maybe longer.

In what turned out to be her last week, she asked me if she had on her white nightgown, and she didn't. She had on a light blue one. I said, "No, I'll get your white one out." I got it out and handed it to her. I think that she could see, but I could tell she was confused. I was very careful to wash and launder that white nightgown about every two days for something like two and a half weeks. She wanted to be sure she had on white.

The priest had come to visit Mom and was with her when her daughter Mary came by. I had called her and said, "Your mother would love to have a visit from you." Mary came and went down the long hall to her room. I had already gone to her room, because she sat up and had a little spell of some sort, and we were freshening her up a bit. Mary came around the corner. I said, "Mom, Mary's coming to visit with you this morning." I know Mom really wanted to see her. Mary took one look at her mother and left. She walked to the front door, opened it, walked down the walk, got in her car, and drove straight down the driveway. I know that's something she wishes she hadn't done.

I was mad, but I felt sorry for her too. That was her mother. They'd been very close. They had lived together a long time. Mom loved Mary. They'd travelled together. They'd reared Mary's two little girls together. They'd shared a house. I guess the last time they'd been together they'd had a kind of falling out, which by that time should have been nothing. If you have a very strong personality, you have a hard time getting around it. We're funny, and we don't react well at times when we wish we had.

The night finally came when our little night nurse came across the house and into our bedroom and said, "I think you and Mr. Hicks better come." When we got to her room, Mom was propped up in bed and didn't seem to realize that George had come into the room. I was careful to tell her, "Mom, George is right there. Put your hand out." We were with her for about an hour and a half. Little by little, her breathing slowed. I patted her shoulder and asked if she was warm enough. I said, "We're just standing right here." She took her son's hand after a while. She died that night, with us on either side of her bed.

The little nurse stayed with her to be sure that everything was done right. She had done that sort of thing before, apparently. Neither George nor I really knew exactly what we should do other than to call and report the death right away.

I remember walking up and down the driveway with George. Soon, daylight began to lighten the pavement, the trees, and the sky. We kept walking up and down the long, winding driveway from our house to Old Hickory Boulevard. George startled me when he said, "Well, you know, I guess I'm an orphan now." That struck me so hard. Here was this big man with so many talents, but we're all little children in the long run. It was sad for him. He had lost his father when he was such a little boy. I say little, but I mean young, because he was quite tall at almost fourteen. And now, he'd lost his mother. He also said, "I guess fifty years is a long time to be alone," which made me think of her in a different light. So we just walked up and down from the house to the road, and back again. Finally the police came, and the coroner, and we took them up to the house and got things done that had to be done.

Mary didn't come by the day her mother died or to the visitation we had at our house, but she came to the funeral. A group of nuns came to say the rosary and then the whole family did it. The funeral was at the cathedral, but I really don't remember it with much clarity. I wish I did. I remember the preamble, certainly. I think I just somehow relaxed.

January 18, 2016

CHAPTER X
Family Life

How George Handled Inconveniences

I have never been able to drive due to the fact that I have only one good eye, and I have problems with that one. I don't have the required depth perception, and it takes me too long to focus. A driver needs to be quicker. But I've been very blessed with wonderful, understanding people who have helped me and our family. My husband George sacrificed an enormous amount of time and effort and things that he would like to have done to readjust his day so that he could do what needed to be done. He did all the grocery shopping, for example. He was much better at that than I was. I went with him frequently, but he took on things that the average young husband should not have had to deal with. I knew perfectly well what an inconvenience it was, but I hoped he understood it when he took me on in the first place. I know he needed to do many things that I couldn't deal with. I never got any discussion about it one way or the other. He was the example for the whole family, and then everybody else, from Judy on down, in one way or another, filled in where I needed help.

Pony Club Dad

George was a heck of a good golfer, really good. For a few years he had the best scores at Hillwood. But as the girls began to ride more and have more success with their ponies, he spent less time on the golf course. He bought a trailer and hauled ponies and children to horse shows and to Pony Club meetings. Our home on Old Hickory Boulevard was in just the right place for a Pony Club family. The Pony Club, in which all the children were involved, except young George, was within riding distance from our house before the golf course was built. They could ride through Percy Warner Park to the meetings where the barn is further down Old Hickory. The park was like our back yard.

My husband never rode horses much, but he ended up being a ringmaster for the Annual Pony Club Show in the park and for lessons when the girls were having instructions. The ringmaster sees that the class runs properly. When a new class is coming in, the ringmaster has to know what the class is and what is required to get the children ready and on time, lined up, and courteously waiting for the judge. He works with the judge to do that. George learned right along with the children.

He had a reputation for pulling the girls out of class immediately if there was any possibility of lightning, even if they were still in the class that was being judged. There's a good deal of metal involved in saddles, stirrups, bits, and iron shoes.

We once lost a horse on our hill, a lovely horse of Judy's named March Wind. Judy would have been maybe a freshman in high school at that point. George fortunately discovered what happened because he knew where he had seen her last, and then all of a sudden he didn't see her after we had a little rainstorm. He didn't tell me, but he quietly left the house and went out and found her. Lightning had struck her when she was standing on the side of a hill, not wearing any metal, and she had been killed. He came in and told me what had happened and got busy on the telephone. He called the company that everybody knew about to have them come and take March Wind away.

George was the one who had to tell Judy. The storm departed as quickly as it had come. The truck had come in, had circled around the hill, and was leaving when Judy came home from school. She didn't get home until 3:30 or 4:00 in the afternoon. It had almost been taken care of, so she didn't have to see any of it. But George had to tell her what happened to March Wind. It was heart-breaking for everybody. That's a sad story, but those things happen, especially if you have horses or other animals in your life.

But we wouldn't have had it any other way. I have mentioned how Judy, as a five-and-a-half-year-old child, went out to the barn way back when we first had ponies, and when she came back, she described Flowers having a baby. That's just the beginning of the whole litany of extremely worthwhile experiences our children had because of their relationships with horses, dogs, and other living creatures that moved through our household. They all learned to accept losses as they come along, whereas it's more catastrophic when you hear about things that happen in nature when you have little connection with it. We had a foal once that died after we'd been taking good care of him. He got his head caught in the cross-link of a fence gate. George found him. I think it was a young colt that had been out with his mother, but evidently he got nosy, as they do, and he got himself caught. That was a sad thing to encounter when going out first thing in the morning.

On the other hand, feeding the foal whose mother couldn't take care of him gave us a happy, tender memory. Everybody was involved with taking care of the horses, and it was a good way to grow up.

A Pony Saunters through the House

We were very fortunate to be in the right place so we could live with so many animals. Everybody had little pets at one time or another. We have had barn cats, house cats, birds, rabbits, and gerbils. We had a science project where we were teaching mice to go through a maze that Sallie had to build herself, so that was exciting. George had something he had to do once with frogs. Then of course, when you are a freshman in high school, you have to dissect a frog. All my children did that.

But the funniest adventure with an animal that we had as a family was the time the children brought a pony in the house. It was mostly Sallie's doing, but everybody was involved. Sallie had a black-and-white pony named Little Bit. He was small, and at six years old, Sallie could handle him well. She'd been riding him since she was four and a half or five.

Most of the children were at home that day. I don't know what precipitated the whole business, but there were enough children at home that one thing led to another, and I heard a lot of activity and went to see what it was. There was a pony in the kitchen. They had brought him in through the back door. I say "they," but Sallie was leading them all. She had a way with animals, and Robin did too. I can't account for it, but they just have empathy and get along with animals of all types. Sallie knew instinctively that what she ought to do with a young foal was to take it everywhere, through our garage, in and around the cars, and everywhere else she could get it to go. She broke the young ponies, and Robin learned to do the same thing by just taking them everywhere. Sallie had brought Little Bit through the kitchen where the floor was, of course, slippery for little hooves. When I encountered them, they were coming through the kitchen and getting ready to turn left to go down the hall past the girls' bedrooms. They did that. There were at least three or four of the girls with her. They were giving the pony quite a tour of the house. There was lots of giggling, lots of carrying on.

They started down the long hall that went past three bedrooms and several bathrooms. This part of the house was all carpeted. They went all the way down the hall. I remember seeing them going all the way down, thinking about that carpet. The walls were painted white and the carpet was bronzy looking. They were getting to the front hall, which was black and white marble which was very slippery. That was about thirty feet they would have walked, at least, down that hall. Then, all of a sudden, somebody yelled, probably not to Robin, who was too young for jumping to, though she was there among them for sure. Somebody yelled, "Grab the tail!" Somebody grabbed the tail and held it up and twisted it, which by their lights, would keep him from soiling the floor. If they were lucky, it would work.

They got him to the front hall and of course his feet were slipping. One of them was standing behind him holding his tail up, and everybody was squealing with pleasure. The whole thing was just ridiculous. They got the front door open and got him out on the front porch whereupon they let go of his tail. I daresay they had been correct to hold up and twist his tail. He did not have a problem inside the house, but as soon as he got to the front porch, he....Well, let's just say he was relieved to be outdoors, finally.

He unloaded on the front porch. But it hadn't been in the hall. He didn't slip and hurt himself at all. He was sliding a little, but he was so relieved to be out of the house, and so were we all. Everybody went for the accoutrements to get it all cleaned up before Daddy got home. I was glad he wasn't home because he would have had to have a discussion with them about this event. But he would have had a terrible time not laughing.

When I first heard the laughter going on and discovered the disturbance, I encountered them making the turn out of the kitchen going down the long hall to go to the front hall. I remember thinking, "Oh my gosh!" But it was fun.

They all helped clean up afterwards. Everybody helped. I remember going to get a trash bag out of the pantry, and then they got it done. They were all used to doing barn work, so that wasn't as awful for them as it might have been for other children. They thought it was pretty awful, but they did it. They had all learned from Pony Club the proper way to clean a stall and how the straw should be banked and all that kind of thing. Not many children need to learn that at six and seven.

This escapade created an enormous amount of laughter.

Garden Party Slingshot

My mother belonged to a garden club, and every spring they had a grand performance that they all worked on. George had expanded our Old Hickory house in the late 1960s, and it had a pool in the middle of it, which sounds a bit grander than it was, but it was fun. We didn't build it till Robin could swim. Everybody wanted Robin to swim and so she was encouraged to be a young swimmer and a good one. It was about thirty feet long and about eighteen feet wide. It was all enclosed. The house, as it happened, was built all the way around it. It had a roof over it, made of sheets of a glass-like material that I think was a kind of plastic. It was about fifteen to sixteen feet high. Harpeth Hall brought girls out in January for Red Cross life-saving lessons because we could heat the pool. I don't think George remembers it particularly well, but he would eat his breakfast and watch the Harpeth Hall girls taking their Red Cross life-saving course. He could sit at the breakfast table and watch that going on. You could see clear across the pool to the other end of the house.

Because it could be heated, the garden-club ladies used the pool as a growing environment for their plants and flowers. For about six weeks beforehand, they were planning their displays. They put the plants they were growing all around the different sides of the pool. The ladies came in and out and in and out almost every day to nurse their plants. Some had flowers; some had other plants, all kinds of things. We had a big collection of caladium. This is what they did for quite a while until the grand performance.

They invited other garden clubs to come. The day the ladies were going to come, there was much excitement. Of course, people from Mother's garden club brought food and served as the hostesses for all this. There was a morning group and an afternoon group. I can't remember the name of the garden club; it was one of the big ones. The children had been warned to pay attention and be prepared for this event. The ladies would come through the front door and go through the living room, but they could put pocketbooks down in one of two bedrooms up and down the hall. They were coming, and we could see them coming. Big George was doing his best to leave. The event was in the early spring, so our children were at school.

Big George was heading for the garage to leave as quickly as he could while this deluge of ladies was coming through the front door. As he was getting ready to leave through the kitchen, he leaned over me. It probably looked as though he kissed me on the forehead, but he was whispering in my ear, "There's a slingshot on the doorknob." Then he disappeared. Only I knew that what he meant. One of the girls had left some of her underwear, always referred to as a slingshot, hanging on a doorknob. If you've got lots of girls in the house, you are apt to have this sort of thing. Our girls were learning to wear bras. I was just thrilled to hear that there was one hanging on a doorknob somewhere, and he was gone. I didn't have time to say, "Which doorknob?" George had the sweetest smile when he left. It created something of a stir. Not many people heard it, but a few people might have known what he meant if they had.

We had a really sweet girl working in the kitchen, and I said to her, "If you can slip down the hall, be looking on the doorknobs on all the bathrooms and the bedrooms because it could be anywhere." We didn't find it until late that afternoon. The ladies had come and gone and admired the caladium, the waterfall, and all the arrangements that had been set up. I only told two friends that were there, "Keep your eye out, we've got a little disgrace going on. See what you can find." And that was the end of it. That's all there was to it. I told Mother later, and she was thrilled to death. She thought that was as funny as could be. This could only happen in a houseful of girls, and only a father would love to go through and mention that, in case you were hoping to have a lovely afternoon.

Babes to Zhivago

I made a list of my favorite movies, and they all turned out to be musicals. *Allegro* was the first one I ever saw in New York that was not Babes in

Toyland, which was really the first one I saw. I liked *Allegro* because it was the first grown-up musical on the stage in New York that I'd ever seen. It was not a success; however, there were songs that I hear every now and again that came from it. One of them was "The Lady is a Tramp," which was fairly popular for a while.

Fantasia was a wonderful movie that Mother took me to see, and I took my children when they were old enough to go. It was not just for children. Through short animated films combined with fine classical music, *Fantasia* attempted to express what music would look like if we could see it. It was kind of a forerunner of things to come in film and music.

I enjoyed the animated animals dancing the "Waltz of the Flowers." The long legged bird with ballet slippers on was just too funny for words. I absolutely loved it. I remember "Night on Bald Mountain." None of my girls remember *Fantasia*. Susan says she remembers being bored to death. I absolutely loved it. I loved the music, and I loved the fact that such great music had been turned into things to see. It was very visual, and, because it was on a big screen, I could see well enough to enjoy it. That's one of the main reasons I love movies in the theater–they are big enough for me to see.

Some of my other favorites are the movie productions of *My Fair Lady*, *The King and I*, and *South Pacific*. I remember the song, "I'm Gonna Wash That Man Right Out of my Hair." What struck me the most about South Pacific was the spoken line, "They have to be taught to hate and fear." This was a veiled reference to the situation on the American mainland right after the war. It made you think a little.

I also enjoyed *The Sound of Music*, which is comparatively recent.

I met the Von Trapp family through friends of ours, a doctor and his wife. These friends bought a house down the road from us. One of the doctor's patients was Maria Von Trapp, who came to see him for trouble with her back and legs. The doctor and his wife had also met at least some of the children.

A friend of mine was so in love with *The Sound of Music* that it was kind of scary. She had seen it at the Belle Meade Theater some thirty times, which bordered on not smart. Nobody needed to see it that many times, though it was very good. When I told the doctor about my friend, he made the arrangements for her to meet Maria. I went with my friend, who was almost sick with excitement to see her. The real Maria was very sweet, very nice, but needless to say, she was not the Maria of the movie. She wasn't Julie Andrews! My friend was terribly disappointed afterwards, but sometimes reality can't live up to our expectations. I don't think she saw the movie again.

All my other favorite movies also turned out to be musicals. There are several songs in *Oklahoma* that stick with me. One is "You can have fun with a son, but you have to be a father to a girl." And he's right. He sang it well with this wonderful big voice. That song always stuck with me. A fun song was "Surrey with the Fringe on Top." That was about a buggy that had "Two bright side lights, winkin' and blinkin'. Ain't no finer rig I'm a thinkin'. You can keep your rig if you're thinkin' that I'd care to swap the shiny little surrey with the fringe on top."

On the more serious side, the movie *Dr. Zhivago* stands out with its beautiful music and Russian setting. George and I saw it twice, I know; maybe more. From *West Side Story*, "A Girl Named Maria" is a particularly memorable song. "Maria, Maria, I just met a girl named Maria." I just loved *Fiddler on the Roof*. Tevye is the name of the man who is in Imperial Russia, and he is wondering if it would spoil some great celestial plan if God could have just made him be a wealthy man. It requires a big man, a rather burly man to sing it, and Zero Mostel was just right for the part.

In the musicals I have loved so much, the composers were able to take certain truths that are essential to understanding the heart of life and express them in words and music so that great numbers of people can take them away in the memory of a song. These musicals are almost little miracles because of how much they give you about what it really means to be alive and have the experiences that we all go through. The melodies affect you so much that you can never get them out of your mind. I always have loved this fact about musicals.

Journeys to Remember

George and I both loved to travel and explore new places, so from the beginning, we went on a variety of interesting trips when we could. The first trip I remember is when we took Judy and Cathy, who were both under five years old, to Mexico. We climbed the steps of some of the ancient pyramids there. Those steps are a lot bigger than they may look in pictures. We had George's mother with us, and she just had a fit about the Mexicans. Cathy was especially blonde, and whenever we were in the streets or in the market, people could not pass her by without reaching out to touch her head and her hair. George's mother kept saying, "*George, George, make them stop doing that!*" Only it sounded like, "*Jarge, Jarge,*" because of her Yankee accent.

Also on that trip, George's mother developed a real affection for rocks. Anytime she passed a rock with a hint of gold in it, she would tell George, "See that rock? I would love to have that one!" He would stop the car, go over and get that rock, put it in the trunk, and get back in and drive on without complaint. And just about every night, he would go out to the car, open the trunk, and take most of the rocks out of the car and put them somewhere so that his mother wouldn't see them again. She did say at one point, "I thought we had a lot more rocks than that." But she did have a large collection, and any more might have made the back end of the car drag along the road.

In Mexico, the flower markets were just wonderful. You could go to the market and buy flowers by the armloads for just pennies. We kept our apartment full of flowers while we were there.

George loved to drive. On at least two occasions, his driving saved our lives. Once when we were on a two lane highway in the mountains of North Carolina, we saw an out-of-control truck coming down the mountain at us. George did everything he could to get us in a safe position, and then he threw himself over me. All of us came out of that event in one piece. I was flattened, but I was able to get back up again.

From the Grand Canyon to Stanford

Taking George to begin college at Stanford became one of our more memorable trips. We wanted him to be able to go to the school he had chosen, but I felt awful about the whole idea of his going to Stanford. We had just had some very bad news about his eyes. He was my little boy, and he was going all the way to the West Coast for college with an eye problem that had to be dealt with. I was not sure George would get the care he needed, and the pressure on his eye was high. We didn't stop him, but we did decide to make the most of getting him there. And if his eyesight was at risk, I wanted him to see some pretty wonderful things before I left him in California.

The most outstanding part of this journey was when big George, little George, and I went to the Grand Canyon. Of course, seeing it was not enough. The two Georges decided to hike down into the canyon together. In one day, they walked down and back. The park rangers do not recommend that people do this. It was a long day for me, and an even longer one for them. Father and son were about the last ones to come back out over the edge of the canyon late in the afternoon. I have never seen two men as tired in my life. I was pretty much worn out, too, because I had had nothing to do but worry while they had their adventure. At dinner afterwards, I was too nervous and they were too tired to talk, so we weren't very good company for each other.

We made our way to Palo Alto and helped George get into his room at Stanford. But eventually all the boxes were unloaded, the bed was made, and our son was ready to start going places and meeting people without his parents. The time comes when you have to shake hands, give a pat on the back, do and say the right things, and go back home. We were standing around in the driveway. My chin always trembled and gave my feelings away. Other parents were shuffling around in the driveway, too, just like us. The boys were thinking, "I wish they would get out of here and go home before somebody falls over and starts crying." George said, "I've got to get your mother to Disneyland. That's where we are going." We got in the car and drove off.

It was a quiet trip to Disneyland. We got to the hotel and went to see things there. I remember trying not to let my chin shake, and I didn't think I could possibly eat. The only thing that helped break the thickness of everything was that I glanced up and saw big George standing there at one of the rides at Disneyland, trying to figure out if he could get into a lavender teacup. That was so ridiculous, that finally I could laugh. Then we were able to go off to dinner.

Stonehenge

Of all the places George and I visited on our many trips, one of the most memorable to me was Stonehenge. We stayed in a house nearby, where we met the owner's English spaniel. This very friendly dog reminded me of Donnie, my beloved dog from childhood. As our new friend squired us around the countryside, he bounded off and came back repeatedly, bringing us a different toy each time, which he must have had stashed away in secret places along the way. We walked together to a charming English pub for our midday meal.

After lunch we went to Stonehenge. Though the day was cold, my heart warmed at the sight of the huge stones so perfectly arranged three thousand years ago. I had lost myself completely in pondering who had moved these stones, and how, and why, when suddenly I heard George say, "Why are you crying?" I didn't know I was. I suppose I was profoundly moved at the thought of what those ancient men had done. From their spirit was born this transcendent monument of wonder and mystery, according to what they, with their primitive means, had been able to learn about the patterns of the stars, the planets, and the seasons. In correspondence with the solstices, they created this harmonious celebration out of impossibly ponderous slabs of stone. I don't know if modern-day people have figured out how they were able to do it. I can't imagine how it was possible.

So George reached into his pocket to see if he could help me with a handkerchief, and found instead a small pile of pink tissues, stamped with pink roses, from our room at the inn. The room had pink wallpaper, a pink bedspread, and pink cushions. The great mystery of Stonehenge is forever married in my mind to those pink tissues from our pink room, and only because my tears moved George to pull them from his pocket for me while we were there. Such unforgettable incongruity on a cold and windswept day, as we stood before that unique, timeless monument which marks with wondrous accuracy the birth of each new year.

February 8, 2016

CHAPTER XI
Forebears & Fellow Travelers

My Mother: Sallie Herbert Read

My mother, Sallie Herbert Read, was born in 1910 to TL and Julia Herbert. Her father was Thomas Levins. He was the third or fourth TL down the line. Mother's birth was interesting. She wasn't her parents' first child. A little boy was born first, TL IV, the one who was a "blue baby." He had a heart defect, which is very simple to correct today, but then, it was not so easily done. He died a little before turning two, a great loss. My grandfather was devastated. He was part of a large family of boys and girls.

When Mother was born, everyone in the family was so grateful, having just lost that little boy, that they had a new healthy and happy baby. As time went on, she developed a bad cough, which they thought was whooping cough, a common early childhood illness then. Her condition was actually asthma, which was serious, but on the whole, she had a very happy childhood.

My grandmother used to tell a story about something that happened to Mother when she was small. She came home from a walk with her nurse and came in crying and said, "Mama, Gertrude said I 'tuck up. I'm not 'tuck up, am I, Mama?" She was very concerned over having been referred to as "stuck up." Not a nice thing for a little girl to be. As it turned out, my grandfather overheard that and made the pronouncement that "It's time for school." I think at the time my mother was barely four.

She started school as a pre-kindergartener. There were times when she was bent over and miserable with her asthma, which of course distressed everybody. Lots of times she would prepare to do something and couldn't because she simply couldn't breathe. As a little girl, I was awakened more than one night to see an ambulance in our driveway and people taking my mother to the hospital again because of her asthma. It's frightening and traumatic for a little girl to see. To my young eyes, Mother was pretty noble then, and to the end of her life. Sometimes she would be desperately ill for days and weeks at a time, but she kept going with enormous courage and determination. She came out of a terrible situation that scared her doctors and everyone to death, but she turned into quite an amazing person. She didn't mind trying different activities and finding out what she could and couldn't do, and she didn't admit defeat easily. That must have been Herbert determination. All the Herberts have it.

Many of her school friends were friends throughout her life. One group of girls with whom she had gone to school way back then ended up forming a luncheon club. They also had a sewing club called "The Sewing Girls." They learned to make baby clothes and all the things that young girls make. They remained staunch friends, being there for each other into their eighties and when they began to die in old age. Friendship meant a lot to her and to each one of them. I knew most of them as a girl and was invited every now and again as a guest to their luncheon clubs at their different homes.

My mother went to Ward Seminary, which became Ward Belmont when I attended and Harpeth Hall for my children and grandchildren. It was a tradition that that was where we went to school.

Aunt Bertha Herbert Potter

What meant most to my mother in her development as a young adult was her relationship with her aunt, my grandfather's baby sister Bertha Herbert Potter, who was quite a well-known artist. She taught my mother how to see with the eyes of an artist. One year in the spring, Aunt Bertha went with my mother to the Ringling Museum School in Sarasota, Florida. They took quite an entourage with them. Aunt Bertha's daughter Patricia (who was a little older than I), the nurse Mattie Battle, the dog, a bird named Sweet, and I all accompanied my mother and Aunt Bertha Potter to Florida.

They took art classes every day. I remember seeing the drawing exercises they were doing. They did some life studies. A number were very routine and basic. Aunt Bertha was beyond that point, but she wanted Mother to start at the beginning, if there is such a thing, to learn to see things. Aunt Bertha could see things wonderfully well. Aunt Bertha did sculpture, which my mother later did, but at first Mother wasn't strong enough. Mother had tiny little hands, tiny little feet. Aunt Bertha was a small person, too, but her hands had become quite strong from manipulating the heavy clay they worked with. In time, Mother began to work with clay in spite of her lack of strength, which she developed, along with quite a bit of skill, because she was so interested in making sculpture. They didn't think about it this way at the time, but working the clay was excellent therapy for my mother, with her asthma.

Mother was fascinated with what Bertha was doing, and Aunt Bertha taught my mother a great deal. Aunt Bertha told me when, at the age of sixteen, I was sitting for a painting a lady was doing of me, that she thought it was amazing what Mother had accomplished and was accomplishing then.

Aunt Bertha was primarily a painter, but she was also a sculptress. She was married to Ed Potter, who was president of a bank in Nashville. Aunt Bertha designed quite a few banks that I see are still using her buildings. They look so different from the ones we're building these days. They were designed in a classical Roman style, or early American classic, meaning red brick buildings, always, preferably with a slate roof and columns, with detailing drawn by Aunt Bertha. She designed a lovely house that is still standing called "Treemont" off Franklin Road, in which Aunt Bertha and her husband and their daughter Patricia lived for several years. She also worked in wrought iron with Philip Kerrigan. Crawling on her hands and knees, she would draw the designs on enormous pieces of paper that unrolled halfway across the room. She designed a fabulous hunt scene that went down the stairway of Treemont, as well as the columns that are still standing on the back of that house. They are quite masterful, very large, and rich in detail. Her communicated vision, the way she conveys space and time in her designs, is quite remarkable.

She also did some perfectly beautiful murals for the semicircular front hall of Treemont. In these murals, life-sized Arabian mares are standing in various positions, massive and exotic looking. When you walk into the space, you gasp because for a moment you think the room is full of beautiful horses. They are slightly larger than life-sized. The Potters had a good bit of land, and they raised horses. These Arabians have a particular look and Aunt Bertha caught them remarkably well. That was the environment that Aunt Bertha offered to the girl who was her niece, her older brother's daughter, my mother Sallie.

Aunt Bertha helped my mother learn to look, see, and appreciate all kinds of things. They went on trips occasionally to New Orleans and had a wonderful time together. Mother learned and loved and grew. She had a sense of color that she helped teach me, because I can see color and it means a great deal to me. She was such a colorist herself that she could transmit her thoughts through color, in painting and with fabric as well. She learned a great deal about a wide variety of artistic media. She was intense, and though at times she was not able to do what she wanted to do, she still pursued every interest with true Herbert tenacity and determination.

How Mother Taught Me

I think my mother was terribly sick when I was born. The whole family was frightened for her for quite some time. As a child I was very conscious of the fact that we took good care of Mother. I had wonderful, sweet nurses and did not lack for anything. But I was aware that my mother was not quite as strong as some of the other mothers I knew. But she made up for her condition, and she made sure I knew how to make up for mine.

Because I couldn't work with books the way other kids did, my mother taught me to read. When we lived in Pewee Valley before I was in school, we spread sheets and blankets out on the lawn, and we would work with flash cards she had made. She had stacks of them, written in a nice black pen, that were purchasable through school supply places. I learned the alphabet in both longhand and the usual printing that you would see in most children's books. They were on different sides of the card. So I learned them both at the same time. We finally learned to build sentences. The sentence might be four feet long. It was done all on the ground, spread out. We built sentences, and built them in both forms of print so I could learn both. So I ended up crawling along on the ground building sentences. It was fun! Mother made it fun. This was quite remarkable, because being out in the grass couldn't have been a joy for her with her asthma. Sometimes she couldn't do it, but we were able to work outside most of the times we tried. But if our dog Jerry lost patience with us, first he would make circles around us; then he would start running; finally, he would get up steam and run right through whatever we were working on, across the sheets and blankets. Cards flew every which way. He ruined our sentences! But that was just part of the fun. Mother would usually just put it all back up, and we would start again. Her patience was incredible.

I didn't much like storms. Our house was on top of a hill with quite a long driveway leading up to it. You could see those summer storms coming from a great distance. If it began to get dark and foreboding, Mother would say, "I think it's time we made fudge." While the storm was coming, we cooked and stewed and made fudge. We cooked the ingredients until they had the right consistency and reached the right temperature. Then we beat it a little bit and poured it out on a buttered platter. Even if it didn't set up quite right, it was still wonderful—we did take a spoon to it occasionally. That was fun too. Now I love storms, because Mother made them mean fudge to me. Bear in mind, my mother was only eighteen when she married, to her parents' distress, so she was still very young when I was a child.

A Fortuitous Meeting on a Train

My father, Robert Read, was not from Nashville, but he was coming to live there for a while when he met my mother. My parents met on a train. I don't know where the train was coming from, but they began to talk on the train, and that's how they made friends. By the time they got off the train in Nashville, they had compared notes, and found that they had friends in common. Daddy introduced the people who were meeting him at the train station to Mother's parents. It was not proper for a lady and a gentleman to meet on the train that way. But Daddy had made all kinds of connections in Nashville. Daddy saw to it that their mutual friends introduced themselves to each other when he first met her. He was determined to become known as an eligible suitor.

My mother's parents must have been terribly upset when Mother and Daddy decided to get married. Mother said that on their wedding day she wasn't sure her father was going to meet her at the bottom of the steps and escort her into the wedding. He did it, but I'm sure he did it with his head down. I frequently remind myself that wedding ceremonies are not always sweetness and light for everybody. They usually work out just fine, but sometimes you just have to get through them.

Whether facing a storm or getting married against her father's objections, my mother made the best of the situation. She didn't pretend there wasn't a problem if there was one; we talked about it, and then we made the best of it. If I have that attitude to any extent, it traces back to my mother. She had such courage. On many a dark night, she sat up leaning over, trying to breathe. This was very frightening because she was not sure she would get through that attack and be able to breathe. She had to stay calm and concentrate on breathing.

She brought that same ability to concentrate to her artistic ability to see, which she taught me. I give a lot of credit for this to Aunt Bertha, because this training was not in Mother's childhood. The more Aunt Bertha spent time with Mother, the more she understood that Mother had the capacity to grow, and she helped her grow and develop as an artist and as a person. They did a lot of things together, and I think Aunt Bertha had more in common with Mother than she did with her own daughter Patricia, though Patricia did eventually turn out to be a lovely artist herself.

Mother's Help with my Schooling

As Aunt Bertha was interested in my mother's learning, my mother went to great lengths to make sure I had the best opportunities to learn. I attended first, second, and third grades at the Anchorage School, just one village up from Pewee Valley. I remember that school very well. The boy that sat in front of me was Charles Norman, a big redheaded boy. I love redheads. He was so nice and I had a lot of affection for him. The boy that I remember so well, but not so fondly, was Burl Hardy. One day he said to me, "Hold out your hand." And I did, idiot that I was. I held out my hand, and he stabbed his sharp-pointed pen into the palm of my hand. I screamed my head off; I'm sure. Of course, there was a big uproar. I had to be taken to the doctor because my hand had to be fixed. I remember that it hurt a lot. I didn't believe anybody would ever do a thing like that. I thought everybody was a friend. That's how narrow my existence was. He taught me something I remembered all my life. Be a little cautious.

After that, Mother went looking for a new school for me. I went along with her.

I needed a school that would be right for me because I had no vision in one eye and limited vision in the other. In grammar school, I usually could not see the blackboard or even what was written on the page in front of me. My mother had good reasons for teaching me how to read by means of flash cards outdoors in the grass before I even started school.

I remember going with my mother up the steps of one school, the school for the blind. I never thought that that school would be appropriate for me, because I could see. I remember sitting in on one class, however, and that the school was big, old, and quiet. The classroom we were in had a great big window. The school did wonderful work; I am sure. Everybody learned to read and write in Braille. I stayed one day. It smelled funny, and the children weren't acting the way I was used to children acting. They were quieter, more polite, and nicer; but it was so dull, and the teacher talked to us rather as if we couldn't hear. (We do have a tendency to talk to people who have some sort handicap or other, and that's not a word I like, as if they are quite dense about things. The fact that a person can't see does not mean he or she can't understand a normal speaking voice.)

When we walked down the wooden steps, down and out of the school, which I remember so well, I was holding my mother's hand firmly. I said, "Mother, are those children dumb?"

"Oh no, don't say that," she said. "That's not the idea. The teacher just wants to be sure they hear everything that she says."

"I don't want to go here."

We got in the car and went somewhere else.

The "somewhere else" we went to was the Louisville Collegiate School. This small school pursued lofty goals in spite of its limited resources. Mother could tell that the teachers there were trying to sharpen their students' intelligence and cultivate a broad understanding of the world in general. They may not have had the training to deal with someone who had a vision problem, but to my mother and me, this school felt right. Mother loved their attitude. Somehow she was able to convince them that I was bright enough to do the work there. They had no way of knowing if I had any sense except for what my mother told them. So that's where my parents sent me. It was the right place at the right time for me.

Sending me there had to require a financial sacrifice for them. As they were both very young, I realize that my Grandfather Herbert probably helped a lot. I think there were only twelve students in a class. That was the largest class for my age. I could still name everyone in my class. It was a super school. I credit them with so much that's good, and when I compare that school and what they wanted us to learn with the school I had just escaped, I am really overwhelmed. My mother said she got a great education herself at Collegiate! I have nothing but gratitude for those decisions that were made on my behalf. Like my mother, Louisville Collegiate did not turn away from a challenge. My good fortune runneth over for sure. I had a great learning experience there until we moved to Pittsburgh after the sixth grade.

They had no reason to take me at Collegiate. I don't remember ever going on an interview there. I have a theory about how my mother convinced them to take me. There's something you must know about my mother. She had this "look." It was practically impossible to turn Mother down when she wanted something. They believed her when she said she wanted them to take me on in their school because she told them so, and then she gave them "the look."

Mother had the most beautiful blue eyes. I didn't know it until I was an adult. (I never know what somebody's eyes look like.) I remember lying with my head in Mother's lap and being quite close to her eyes. Occasionally when the light was just right, I realized that she had blue eyes. I learned later that they were wonderful. If she looked at you and she put that Herbert glare on you, you knew a powerful force was being focused on you. My children always said, "Grandmother is wonderful, but if she gives you the look, there's no doubt you're going to give in." No point in discussing it. She did it very softly, very gently. My mother was always a lady; she really was. They would all tell you that. Grandmother was very seldom cross, but if she gave you the look, it was all over. Susan has often said, "I look in the mirror and I try to get Grandmother's look. It would be so useful." All the children agree. Grandmother had a look. She probably never turned it on you more than two or three times in your life, if that much. She wouldn't need to.

Collegiate was rare. In every conceivable way, it was a growth experience for all of us, every last one of the twelve of us in my class. How they found a spot for me, I don't know. Many things that were required for me to do, I couldn't do. But somehow I got through. The credit goes not to me, but to them. They understood that you can't do more than your best, and my best was quite limited. The teachers there stimulated our sense of beauty and encouraged us to use our imagination. Overall, the school had a courteous, English atmosphere. It was both strong and gentle. The attitude, demeanor, and intentions of Collegiate made an imprint on me, and I've never forgotten it.

Winchester Thurston

When we moved to Pittsburgh, I went to Winchester Thurston. It seemed as though most things about living in Pittsburgh were lessons in learning to adapt to a completely different environment, and school was no exception.

I am sure my mother met with the school administration before I went for my interview. She would have done her best to explain what I could and could not do. But I pretended that I could do things that I couldn't really do and got away with it at the time, so she wouldn't have known fully my abilities in all subjects. My mother read many assignments aloud to me, and some of them were quite long. She claimed that my assignments were the best part of her education.

When we were in Pittsburgh, I had what was thought to be rheumatic fever. I missed about a month and a half of school. Mother and I were together at home a lot in the dark of the long, cold winter. She had some problems with her asthma, but being unwell at the same time brought us very close. We read together in those months. I read to her more than usual, because her asthma made it hard for her to read aloud, and then we talked about what we were reading.

We talked about things we liked to look at and places we had been that we particularly liked. We were kind of like two girls together. She was worried about me, but I was worried about her because that particular period of Pittsburgh was pretty unattractive. They had rented a house in what was called Squirrel Hill, an ugly eastern house. It had some stained glass windows, heavily leaded with orangey yellow and an ugly shade of red glass. They were so ugly that they were funny. The living room had windows in all the wrong places with awkward, built-in cabinetry. All in all, we picked that poor house apart in our own heads and aloud. My mother had the ability to make something attractive, but if it couldn't be beautiful, she could make it funny. We would set up little vignettes. If this wasn't there, and that was thus and so, and we could magically change it all, what would we change? So we reconstructed the house imaginatively.

When they finally let me out of the bed for a while, we would go to town. Later in the year, when my legs weren't hurting so much, we went to Kauffman's, a big store there, and to several others a few times just to get out and do something different. We did as much as we could together, and we grew together. In that year, I matured and became better company for my mother. The time of bonding with my mother during that year, like everything I have experienced, was a special gift to both of us. It came at just the right time.

Mother became to me like a homeschool teacher, but she put her foot down on one matter: "I cannot teach you math." That was the end of that. My father could have taught me the math, but he was gone too much with his work.

Because of some of the good things I have mentioned, the period in Pittsburgh was not quite a black hole.

Back to Nashville for Ninth Grade

At the end of the year, when it snowed on my birthday, May 19, I chose that moment to tell my parents that I wanted to go south. I am not sure what went on behind the scenes, but my parents made a plan with my mother's parents in Nashville. Ward Belmont was a girls' school in Nashville, and it took boarders as well as day students. I enrolled in the school for the next fall. The plan was for me to go as a boarder, and my mother, who had been sick a lot because of the polluted Pittsburgh air, would come to Nashville for long parts of the year and stay with her parents. I could sign out often and spend weekends with my grandparents. My father would have to stay in Pittsburgh because he was needed by Alcoa. His work as assistant treasurer was considered to be an important part of the war effort because Alcoa was producing many items for the American and British military. My mother ended up coming sometimes, but my parents stayed in Pittsburgh for almost two more years. My mother really needed to get out of Pittsburgh with the harsh winters and the dirty air. It's hard to believe how bad the air was then, since it is perfectly lovely there now.

As far as Mother was concerned, she had a lovely period of coming home to Nashville when they did move back here. Then she could be herself. She was not "on" all the time with responsibility for me, and she was happy to be at home. She reconnected with all her wonderful old friends.

Her life didn't change a great deal until after George and I were married, and our children came along. When my children began to show up, it was a whole new world in many ways for her, because she loved every last one of them. When Judy was born, Mother was the first person to arrive at the hospital. She adored Judy just as soon as she was born. She was so proud of everything that Judy did from the first step she took. Then Cathy had tea parties with my mother. She had many different kinds of lovely encounters with the children.

She was an angel about doing what I couldn't do. Since I didn't drive she drove them to many of the places they needed to go. My father was concerned about her. He said, "You don't realize how much time that takes out of your mother's life." Without being rude, I tried to say, "But you don't know how much she enjoys it." At least she succeeded in making me think she did. It was hard for Daddy, then, too, because he had come back to Nashville after that really important job in Pittsburgh. He was getting reestablished with several friends to open a company here, and Mother was engrossed with the babies. She couldn't enjoy me when I was a baby, goodness knows. She was too sick. Although her asthma continued to trouble her, the fun was beginning to come with grandchildren.

Now it's true that she hadn't anticipated that we would have so many, but the fact is, Judy was just the love of her life. Then little blond Cathy was so gentle and sweet. Sallie she loved because she thought Sallie looked so much like me as she remembered me as a little child. She was fascinated with George. She worried so about him because he was born with the same problem I had, but she had never had a little boy, and I think she particularly loved him. Then when Susan and Robin came along, it was just unbelievable that they were here. "They had the boy! Why in the world have any more?" I understood how my parents felt.

Grandmother Read

I was happy we were able to name Susan for my Grandmother Read. She had just lost her husband a month and a half before Susan was born, so it really cheered her up when we named Susan after her. It had meant so much to George and me, and also to my mother, that when we got married, Grandmother Read took her first airplane ride to come to our little wedding, which was unbelievable generosity. I also think naming Susan helped my father, Robert Read, because he was mourning the loss of his father. Mother and Gran had always gotten along amicably, but they lived in two different cities and they didn't know each other very well.

Grandfather Herbert

I don't think Grandfather Herbert ever saw the Collegiate School, but he trusted Mother's judgment about it, so he supported my going there. He also directly handled a significant aspect of my education himself. He taught me some things that have stayed with me forever about how to treat people. I guess he understood me better than I thought, which I didn't realize until much later.

He had a large brick-making company and sold brick all over the South. His grandfather was a Bush who owned the Bush Brick Company. In my grandfather's time, Bush Brick evolved into the TL. Herbert Company. The T was for Thomas, and the L was for Lemuel. My grandfather was called simply TL.

As a child, he had had a lot of trouble with his legs. His best buddy when he was growing up was a black boy named John Douglas. My grandfather's family owned orange groves in Florida. His family often visited these groves, which was where John grew up. When they were about eleven or twelve, my grandfather and John did many things together. In time, John went to work for my grandfather's company. My grandfather travelled a lot. He did not see well, so John did the driving. Grandfather Herbert took me on trips quite a bit when I was out of school, and John drove. In these outings, my grandfather taught me what he wanted me to know about the world.

He thought girls ought to have all kinds of experiences, just like boys. He made sure I saw things I never would have seen. He was by no means easy to travel with, but he was a real educator.

He had a forty-foot boat that he kept in Pensacola, Florida. As a child, I always thought that it was my grandfather's boat, but I think it probably belonged to the company. I went down every spring break, and we did a lot of cruising around Florida. We would go down and get on the boat and cruise. A forty-foot boat is not great big, but it was nice. I think it slept eight. He always docked somewhere interesting and different.

He liked to go out on the docks where the fishing boats were coming in. Because he wanted me to meet all kinds of people, he took me to see where the Greek sailors came in after a day of sponge fishing. They were entirely different people from anyone I had known. We went on board and joined them for meals. In the car on the way back home I once said, "I feel so sorry for these people. This is such a hard life." He said, "Don't ever pity anybody. You don't mean to do it, but you are diminishing them. These are very worthy and good people, and they are working hard."

The muleskinners at the brickyard had also earned great respect from him. A great deal of that labor was done with the help of mules, which pulled big pallets of brick around. I saw him talk to all sorts of people. He showed an interest in everybody. It was an education to go somewhere with him and watch his relationships with the people who worked for him.

Grandfather Herbert often surprised me. He was not particularly wedded to doing things a certain way. He'd go to New York to visit connections and friends in the ladies' clothing business, and he would buy the most beautiful handmade French lingerie. You never knew what he knew. He would give mother a dozen stockings at Christmas with a lovely hostess gown. He chose the most beautiful things.

He was a very hard worker himself. It was a real experience whenever I was with him, and I absolutely adored him. But he was kind of a challenge sometimes, too. I think he was kicked out of two high schools when he was young. Then as an adult, only John could have been his chauffeur because he'd say, "Let's try that; I've never been there!" And soon, they would be off. He had a passion for new experiences.

He treated the people who worked for him with a great deal of respect. He could be tough about the job, but the man he respected. He said, "They do something I can't do. Learn to see the whole picture as much as you can." He is saying this to an eleven year old. I remember those lessons. I value them more now than I did at the time. He was quite different from my father in many ways, but he and my husband got along very well. It was funny to see them standing next to each other. George was six feet four and my grandfather was not very tall, but they had a lot in common. George also knew how to work with men, since he worked in construction. They both taught me lessons I couldn't learn from anyone else.

He thought my mother was absolutely wonderful. He'd lost a child, and then this little girl came along and gave him delight and joy that helped him recover from the grief over the little boy he had lost. Although Mother wasn't quite well enough to go on many little jaunts with her father when she was a girl, he taught her, too, as he did me, by going places and doing things with her as much as she could go and do. Lessons learned from my grandfather were part of my education that was certainly as important as school, and perhaps more foundational, because what I learned with my grandfather is in my blood.

He added a dimension to my understanding of the world that nobody else could have done, so I am extremely grateful to him. I know that's what went into my mother, too. I know her tenacity. Even though she was not well, she was thinking all the time. Her father's influence and teaching are behind her ability to see and do. His efforts connected with the way Aunt Bertha taught her to see the world. Then my mother passed her perspective on to me, as much as I could swallow. I have so much to give thanks for.

Grandmother Herbert

My Grandmother Herbert, Julia, was the musician. It was disappointing that I was not one, but she did her best to make sure I at least got to hear good music. She was not a beauty, but she was a wonderful pianist. She played with the Louisville Symphony Orchestra on several occasions, and some of her compositions are in the archives of Kentucky, her home state, including "Love's In My Heart." She was friends with Grace Moore, Lily Pons, and other accomplished musicians of her day. To her grandchildren and great grandchildren, she was known as "Nanny." My husband George just loved her. She was involved in the Nashville music scene, but she would also go to the opera in Atlanta and went frequently to New York to visit her friends in the music world. She was very familiar with New York.

When we went to New York for my surgeries, as we did several times, she would sometimes go with us. We would stay in the Sulgrave Hotel on Sixty-seventh Street near Park Avenue in Manhattan. It was a small, gracious hotel with a little garden area beside it where you could have meals in decent weather. That sort of thing was rare in New York even in those days. Once when we were staying there, she went out for a morning appointment and came back much later, completely exhausted. It turns out that after her morning appointment, she got in a cab to come back to the hotel, and when it came time to tell the driver where to take her, she went totally blank. She had a senior moment. I have had a few, so I know how that's very possible. So she apologized to the cabbie and said, "I have changed my mind. I think I want to walk a little." She got out of the cab started walking back. She knew exactly where she was and where to go; she just couldn't find the words for the address or the name of the hotel, which was a long way from where she was.

When she finally arrived at the hotel, the doorman told her, "Why, Mrs. Herbert, you look like you have been running a mile!"

She said, "I almost did." She came into the hotel, went upstairs, ordered coffee, and collapsed. Finally, she told my mother that she had walked back from her appointment. My mother asked her how far she had walked. They got out a map, and my grandmother showed Mother where she had started. It turned out she had walked over fifty blocks, which in New York City is around two and a half miles. She had tiny little feet, with short legs, and she moved fast. For a lady in her early sixties who had had broken and sprained her ankles on several occasions, this was quite a long distance for her to walk; but what disturbed her most was that she couldn't find the words to tell the cab driver where she wanted to go. Nobody could believe that she had walked over fifty blocks. She never walked any distances if she could avoid it. Everyone who knew her realized that must have been quite an ordeal for her, but she came through it with the determination that was customary for her. After that, Mother was always careful to see that she had her address written down and with her whenever she went anywhere.

Her determination and her love of music combined on one unforgettable occasion. In 1939, the great singer Marian Anderson had been denied permission to sing in Constitution Hall by the Washington, D.C. Chapter of the Daughters of the American Revolution because she was black and they had a rule against integrated audiences. This mistreatment of the great musician and lady made Grandmother Herbert so angry that she bought tickets for me, my mother, and herself to see Marian Anderson sing at the Syria Mosque when we lived in Pittsburgh. She made the trip from Nashville to Pittsburgh and back just to take us to this concert. I was prepared to be impressed, and I was awestruck with the woman's remarkable voice. She had a striking personal presence as well.

What Grandmother Herbert passed on to me was punctuality. I learned from her to detest being late. I don't mind if somebody else is late, but I'm not nice about being late myself. It disturbs me considerably. That's because I have so often seen Grandmother being beyond punctual. She usually was ahead of everybody else. If she was to meet someone at 10:00, she was there at ten minutes until 10:00. Some people found that side of her annoying, but being early was a good habit for a musician to have.

My Grandmother Herbert and my husband George played canasta very seriously. Many a date found me sitting on a sofa with a new magazine while George and Nanny played out their canasta game. They hit it off very well, and whether or not my parents were enthusiastic about George, Nanny certainly was. They were always great friends.

My Mother in Her Later Years

My mother had never lived in a house when she was growing up. Her father was so afraid of fire that their family always lived in hotels throughout her childhood. As an adult, she developed a strong interest in houses and architecture. My mother was mostly self-taught, but if she had been stronger, she could have made quite a career for herself out of interior decorating and design.

When George was developing the lots on Herbert Place (named for my mother's family) and Georgian Place between Chancery Lane and Chickering Road, my parents bought a very pretty lot from George on Georgian Place. My mother and George worked together on the plans for this house. It was a delicious house. There were no two ways about it. It was in a classic French style, with tall French windows and tall ceilings in the drawing room. My mother created very extensive gardens around the house, and she and my father enjoyed many happy years there together. After my father died, we all agreed that Mother should come and live with us, so we built a room for her in the house at number 10 Middleton Park on the front southeast corner of the house. It had high ceilings, French doors, and the black marble mantelpiece from our old house, with oyster silk-lined curtains, full and billowy. Everything was beautifully put together.

She didn't want to have a bed in her sitting room, so she found a full-length, Italian, white-and-gold daybed, the width of a single bed, with cushions all across the back. When you walked in to the room, the feeling was that that was a very comfortable sofa. The pillows could be removed at night, and she slept on the bed.

There was a lovely tea table that I now have in front of the fireplace in my living room. The chairs were Louis XVI for the most part. The colors were subtle and lovely, but the jewels of the room were found in her art collection. The painting that is now over my mantle, in which, if you look at it carefully, every stroke is interesting, was over her bed. Ten or twelve small and medium sized oil paintings hung against the dark gold walls, which themselves were painted in a lovely fern-like design. The tea table stood by her chaise lounge. Her desk was a nice, large Louis XV bureau plat. I still have it now. All of it together made a beautiful room.

Carolyn, a wonderful character on her own, came with Mother when she came to our house. When she came to apply for a job at the old house before it was sold, she arrived in a copper and gold Cadillac of the current year. She loved to drive my mother wherever she needed to go. She and my mother were great friends. They went shopping together and ran their errands. She had an opinion about most things, and as Mother used to say, "You know, she is often right! She is often very right!" She was very particular about how to set up Mother's tray for dinner. She prepared many of Mother's meals in the little kitchenette, which was close to Mother's room. She insisted that there was to be a butter knife on the tray. She took extremely good care of my mother. When she was driving, she was always careful to have on a white uniform. She took meticulous notes about mother's medications. Having Carolyn was like having a really good guardian angel that you could see and hug.

Carolyn once told me, "Mrs. Read saved my marriage. She helped me understand what the problems were, and I will be indebted to her all my life." There was nobody like Carolyn. We couldn't have been more blessed.

Fellow Travelers and Helpers

Throughout the years, many wonderful people have been helpers and fellow travelers for us along the way. John Douglas began as a companion and helper for Grandfather Herbert when they were both young boys on the family's orange groves in Florida. Years later, he worked for my grandfather at W. G. Bush and Company. As my grandfather's chauffeur, he helped pick out the cars and take care of them. Like me, my grandfather didn't see very well, and John saw that everything went right. He was very important to all of us. When my mother was twelve, John taught her to drive. My grandfather's company bought John Douglas a nice little white house, where he and his wife lived with their adorable daughter named Princess, and Princess was a little "'tuck up," I might add. When she got older, she went to college. I remember that John drove me to some of my special events. When I was younger, my grandfather took me on business trips with him, and John drove us wherever we went. I loved being with John.

Late-Night Giblets

John Douglas was involved in many aspects of my grandfather's business and personal life. He was the most trustworthy, wonderful man. I remember once when my grandfather brought me along on a trip to a college. My grandfather would have John just drive and drive until he said, "That is enough. We'll stop here. We know where we're going to be in the morning." We were passing through somewhere like Michigan when he decided he was tired, and he thought I was. So he asked John to find us a hotel. It was late when John got me into a room, but then he realized that we really hadn't had any dinner. He said, "Now, Miss Sallie, you go ahead and get ready for bed, and I will bring you something to eat." Then he disappeared. It was 1:00 or 2:00 in the morning, and bless his heart, not many places to eat could have been open that late.

A while later I heard a knock on the door. It was John, who said, "I didn't do very well Miss Sally, but see how this is." I think it was a giblet sandwich. I don't know where in the world he could have gotten it, but he was doing the best he could. It wasn't his fault that my grandfather stopped us in a bad spot. The hotel was all right; it was little, but it was okay. I could not eat that sandwich, and I knew it. I remember trying to divide it up into pieces. I said to myself, "I'd better flush it." I really didn't want to disappoint John, and he couldn't have done any better. There was no choice in that place at that time, and I don't know how hard he had to look to find what he found.

I hoped that the plumbing worked well. I divided the sandwich into small sections and got rid of it. I guess every time I flushed the john, hoping another piece of the giblets sandwich would go down, everybody else thought, "Somebody's really sick!" I went to bed hungry, but not as hungry as if I had eaten that giblets sandwich.

I have no idea what, or if, my grandfather had anything to eat that night. We could have stopped somewhere better earlier, but he didn't care much about meals. Years later, I eventually found the courage to mention the presence of hunger at times, but no word about that giblet sandwich ever passed my lips.

Ellen, Eleanora, Ruth, and Catherine

Ellen did housekeeping and cooking for my Grandmother Herbert when I was little. She let me shell peas in the kitchen. She taught me to put thumbprints in the cookies she made; then she'd go along behind me with a demitasse spoon, putting jelly in the thumbprint. I can taste them now. She also made the most delicious stuffed red snapper, by the platter full, so everyone loved to go there for dinner. She was a warm, sweet person who hummed all the time she was cooking. Ellen was kind of plump.

John brought her every morning. When they were in season, she would bring fresh peaches for my grandfather. She would peel and serve them for breakfast with his shredded wheat. Isn't it funny the things you remember? John would choose the fresh peaches and give them to Ellen. I can see it just as plain as if it were happening right now. Those were just everyday things that still live in my memory.

Eleanora worked for my parents when I was a child. She moved with us to Louisville and kept house for about two years to get Mother all settled with a child and a new town, and then she went back to Nashville.

Then there was Ruth, who did the laundry. She was quite young but she learned to be a very good cook. Her husband Charlie made friends with our grumpy dog Jerry and gave him a bath once a week. He did a little of everything. He always saw what needed to be done and did it in the nicest, quietest way. My mother did a little oil painting of Charlie, but somehow it's been lost, to my great sorrow. I remember he was in a yellow shirt as he sat for her. Then they had a son, Little Charlie, and Mother did an oil sketch of him and gave it to Ruth. So she has that, and I don't have the one of Charlie, and I wish I did because it was quite good.

There were lots of people in between. Ruth was the one that got me down off the jungle gym when I went up one morning early and got stuck and wasn't sure how to get down. I went up all by myself and got in trouble. It wasn't that high, so she could reach up and have me lean over, and she pulled me down. She was my savior! I don't know how long I would have sat there. She was a long, tall lanky girl, and really sweet. Later she had a baby, a little girl with pigtails that she would bring up to the house in a red and white dress and a white pinafore. Cutest thing you ever saw. That child would sit on a stool in the kitchen and just be so patient and sweet.

Of course, John Douglas was always there. He would drive my grandfather up to Louisville. They were always together. I heard that my grandfather would walk out of a hotel that wouldn't let John stay in the room with him because he helped him dress and undress. Sometimes the hotel would take an attitude that they didn't want that Negro in there. So my grandfather would just pick up and say, "We're leaving."

"Oh! Oh, Mr. Herbert, you always stay here!"

"I don't think I will in the future." And off they'd go.

There was Catherine that I stomped my foot at and got a spanking for. That was on Derby Day. I learned a lesson from my father. I said I wouldn't wear a sweater and he came back and heard me tell Catherine that I wouldn't wear a sweater and that started the whole thing. It was one of the few paddlings I ever got, but I got that one.

Nadine and Roscoe

After George and I had married and started our own family, Nadine was with us to care for young George and Sallie and the others. She was sweet, pretty, loving, and girlish in a way that made it seem she was younger than she was. She took such good care of George. She had had some eye surgery herself, so her heart went out to that little boy. George and Sallie were about the same height when they were in their twos and threes, and Nadine loved them and played with them and taught them all kinds of good things. She was the very soul of patience.

Every time she heard that my mother might stop off during the afternoon for some reason, she would get Sallie and the older girls dressed up to meet their grandmother. She always brought a pot of tea into the living room even if it was blistering hot; it didn't matter. She thought it wouldn't be suitable not to serve tea to Grandmother. She was the happiest person and very important to our family. She loved holidays and did a lot of the things that Cleo, who is here now, does for us on holidays.

When I went to the hospital to have our son George, Sallie was almost two. Nadine spent the night and was a nervous wreck until we finally got word that George had arrived. Oh, she was glad to see that baby boy! "Ah, Mrs. Hicks, he's got red hair!" She thought that Sallie and George were hers. They were certainly the luckier for it because she enjoyed them.

Nadine and Roscoe were married, but they weren't sure we would approve, so they tried to keep their marriage hidden from us. Finally, the secret came out that they were married. We were delighted! That was just fine with us.

Roscoe worked with big George. He did almost everything that you could think of. The two of them cleared the land and built a barn. Roscoe built the fences, but they painted them together. Both of them were very hard workers. They would be out there working in the hot sun and would not stop to rest, so I used to bring iced tea to them out in the fields just to get them to take a break. By the time George and I went on our last trip to Europe, Nadine was working part-time at a florist's shop. She'd call me once every two or three weeks and tell me how she liked the florist business. When she and Roscoe heard that George had died, they came to the house with two big trays of Nadine's wonderful homemade rolls. I didn't see them; somebody told me later that Nadine and Roscoe had come. I was sick because I really wanted to see them. They meant so much to us. When it was necessary, Roscoe drove every now and again for me. They were two of the nicest, warmest, sweetest most considerate people you'd ever want to know.

Willie B, Susie, and Mattie

Willie B worked for my mother first. He would come once a week and do whatever needed to be done. Willie B could always figure out how to do it. We had a barn party once when Judy was in high school, and he dressed up in a costume and served food for the guests up in the hay loft. Willie B loved dressing up for that party, and his picture was in the paper for that party. He wore a chef's hat and a scarf around his neck and a big apron. He waited on all the kids. He added so much to the party because he really entered into it and enjoyed it so much himself. He was always called Willie B. Mother always thought it meant "Will he be here?" because sometimes he wasn't. A good gardener, he worked for Mother primarily, but he worked in the house too. He worked at our house some. He could really polish silver; he rather liked doing that.

Then there was Susie who worked in our first house on Old Hickory and helped take care of George's mother when she was with us. She helped George's mother bathe and dress and lots of personal things. She fixed her lunch so that she felt a little independent and not as much having to deal with us. She didn't drive. Susie was a lovely woman. Her husband worked at the Belle Meade Club golf course as a greens keeper.

I skipped Mattie Battle way back at the beginning. She was my cousin Patricia's nurse. Mattie pretty much raised us until we were five or six. She taught me to write my name as I sat in a little chair at a table on the sun porch on the second floor of Aunt Bertha's house in Nashville. Mattie was in charge of Patricia and me. John Douglas drove us, with Mattie, to

Sarasota, Florida, when Mother and Aunt Bertha went to the Ringling Museum School.

These people wove in and out of my childhood. They were so important to me because they took care of me and taught me so much.

Mattie was such a lady. Not long ago I was at Centennial Club and a lady came up to me that I didn't know and she said, "Are you...?" and I admitted to it. She said, "Didn't Mattie Battle take care of you and your cousin when you were little?"

"Absolutely," I said.

Well, evidently a woman named Emma had worked for her parents as she was growing up, and Emma and Mattie were sisters. They were both Battle girls. So it's funny the interconnections that you have in Nashville. She was telling me all about Emma, and she knew that Mattie Battle had gone with us to Florida.

Mattie was deeply kind and sweet. She always wore a white uniform, but she had things in tow because she was pretty much in charge when we were very small. I remember once when we were in Montgomery, Alabama, and John stopped for us to have lunch. He understood about lunch! He went in and told the management that Mattie was coming with these two little children and that they would need a table in the big dining room. I remember that dining room with its great big ceilings. It must have been in a hotel. John walked the little dog, Fluff. Patricia had a little dog that travelled with us, as well as her canary. He saw to it that they understood that Mattie was to sit with us. Aunt Bertha had written to the effect that Mattie was in charge of these children. They were not very happy about having her come in, but she was careful always to wear a nurse's outfit, and she had two little girls by the hand. They put us as close to the kitchen as they could but left us in the dining room. We were nicely waited on, but they were prepared for somebody coming in and saying, "What's that ____ doing in here?" It must have been awful to have to live through that. These were the most responsible people in the world. I don't know how they could have been so nice.

John ate many a meal in the car; I can tell you that. I saw that, and it made me furious. Mattie ate at the table with us. I didn't read the note, of course, but I believe Aunt Bertha made it clear that the children were not to be left alone at all. Mattie was in charge of their manners and so forth. I think she probably made it clear. I was too young to understand what was going on, and yet I sensed it, though I didn't know how to process it. On the other hand, every now and again, people would stop by the table and speak to us, often to admire Patricia's beautiful yellow corkscrew curls, of which I was very jealous. I'm here with bangs and short, dark hair. I absolutely adored her, and I knew she was absolutely beautiful. So there was this pair of little girls sitting there with Mattie, who was beyond plump and in a very white starched uniform and as proper as she could be. She was instructing us in our table manners and seeing to it that we behaved well. One lady stopped off and chatted with Mattie. She told them we were from Nashville and where we were going. John Douglas negotiated us in and out of several situations like this.

Cleo

Cleo came when I broke my femur. After about one day, I had had enough of the convalescent place, so Susan and Sallie decided I was leaving, and they came and got me. They began looking for someone to take care of me, and Cleo was recommended to them.

She came over Thanksgiving. She thought we were so funny. Susan was trying to put a turducken that a neighbor had given us in the oven, but my roaster was so big she couldn't close the oven door; so they just pushed it in as far as it would go, and then closed the door as much as they could, put a chair up against the door, and sat in the chair. Cleo thought we were the funniest thing she had ever seen. She has a marvelous sense of humor. She has been with us now about fifteen years.

She does not like dogs in the house and doesn't believe they should be there. The idea of touching fur is almost beyond her. Bless her; she puts plastic gloves on when she takes Murphy out for a walk. She has gotten pretty fond of him, but she still doesn't want to touch him. She knows all the children and all the grandchildren. She has been widowed since about the time I broke my leg, and that was why she was available when we found her.

The other day, she brought in a platter with angel food cake, strawberries, and whipped cream; and that was my lunch. It was absolutely all I could deal with. She takes very good care of me. Sometimes she is a little grumpy, but not for long.

Cleo has two nieces who were going to be baptized, and I wanted to give them something, so I wrote Cleo a check, and she took them to St. Mary's Bookstore, which was quite an interesting place for them. Each chose a bracelet, and they wrote me the sweetest thank you notes. The owner of St. Mary's called later to tell me, "Those were the cutest girls!"

These are wonderful, rare people who meant so much to me growing up. I got indoctrinated when very young about people I love, and I obviously don't care what their skin looks like. I know kindness through and through. So it's affected me always. I'm not going to battle, I guess due to cowardice, though at times I almost thought I should. It wouldn't have changed anybody's attitude, but I carry mine with me. It has to do with these sweet people that were kind and patient, who taught me so many things and were so reliable and so good. I don't take kindly to a lot that I see around me among some people in the South, and it makes me very unhappy. It is no consequence because I don't do much of anything to help anybody. I know I don't know enough, but I know what I know, and what I know is there are wonderful, warm, sweet godly people out there that must make God smile quite often. I have been very blessed to be close enough to a lot of them. I'm grateful that I grew up the way I did. I didn't learn a thing in Pittsburgh, at all, not a thing. I'm at home in the South and love the South. But I hate to hear some of the people I am fond of take attitudes that I know are wrong. There are people whose hearts are so big and who care for others so much. I am really overwhelmed with the angels that we encounter and don't realize what good, long-suffering, sweet, patient, dear souls we get to meet.

February 22, 2016

CHAPTER XII
Looking Ahead

Thanksgivings to Come

On this April day, in my last month as an 86-year-old, I have just realized all the wonderful things I have to look forward to between now and the end of November. If I can list them all, it will give a good clear picture of what a marvelous family I have been so grateful to be part of for a long time now. There's just a lot on this old lady's plate, and it all has to do with my children, grandchildren, and great-grandchildren. I want people to know how much all of these events mean to me.

Starting with April, my daughter Susan's birthday is this month.

Then we move into May, which is Steeplechase month. I believe my grandson Gustav Dahl, who just turned 21, has three mounts to ride in the Steeplechase, which he has done before. Robin called recently to tell me he has just won three races. These are the kind of races where the horses jump over fences while running around the track. It's very competitive and there are some risks involved. I've gotten so I almost try not to worry. I can't say I completely don't, but Gustav has been a very competent rider since he was a very young boy. He used to go fox-hunting with Robin at an early age. He's had a couple of mishaps that would have kept me out of the saddle forever, but he bounced back rather quickly. He has an excellent attitude and deep love of racing. Plus, he's quite good at it.

I've spent many second Saturdays in May on the hill watching our Steeplechase, which is one of the very oldest in the country. I am sorry to say I can't make the hill anymore, but I never dreamed of having a grandchild racing in it. Television does not cover it well except for the last race, but I've got somebody on the telephone giving me a rundown the whole time. We've had the same box for many, many years, and now the grandchildren and all the cousins use the box. It's not big enough for all the cousins, but they work it out among themselves every year. Whoever is going to be here this year, I know the box will be full. There will be eight Hickses in that box.

About the same time we have a grandson due to be born in Atlanta. Cathy's daughter Natalya Davis will be having a baby boy. He has an almost-two-year-old big sister who is looking forward to him. She knows that she is getting a brother, and he is, I think, going to be named Alexander, provided that he looks to his parents like an Alexander once he arrives. There's always the possibility that the baby will come and the name doesn't fit, and there have been name changes at the last minute on occasion. Alexander is kind of a long name for his sister, so she's calling him "Zander." I'm looking forward to meeting him in a big way. He will probably stay in Atlanta for at least a month, but I will get to meet him, I hope. Fortunately, Atlanta is close, so he and his mother and sister will be here fairly often during the summer, and I am looking forward to meeting him. That's May.

In June, George's son Thomas will turn nine, and my youngest daughter, Robin, who has been widowed for about three years, is marrying Mike Owen at a little garden wedding on June 11. So we just ordered the wedding cake. That will be at a close friend's house. Almost everybody will be there. Gus is going to stay after the Steeplechase until the wedding. Robin will be attended by her daughter Rachael and the groom, whom I am very fond of. He's a sweet person and I can't think how lucky we are to have him joining the family. Robin's two sons, Gus and McClain, will be on either side of Mike. It's going to be a small wedding, but not that small, as the list is growing. I am excited about that and hope I can maneuver in the garden because I certainly intend to be there one way or the other. And that's June.

Robin's birthday is in July. In August we have several birthdays, including McClain's. There are several birthdays in September, too. Then things quiet down for a while.

A November Wedding

We have a big wedding coming up in Memphis over Thanksgiving weekend. Everybody will come from everywhere. Susan's son John is marrying Sarah Stringfellow, from Memphis. The wedding will be in Memphis on Thanksgiving weekend. That's a good weekend for our family because the long weekend gives all our people time to get there and back. John's sister Sallie is going to be a bridesmaid for Sarah. We seem to stick with certain names, like Sarah and Sallie. John's friends from high school and college will all take part on his behalf. So there will be a big movement toward Memphis that weekend.

I have said that I would like to contribute the wedding cake, so the bride and her mother are supposed to meet with the caterer and the baker from Memphis. I'd love to have the cake made by our superb baker here, Leland Riggan, who has done wedding cakes for us forever; but I don't begin to think we could transport it from here to Memphis. Sarah and her mother know the cake maker in Memphis that they want, so they will be planning that. This is a rather serious matter. They do sketches and decide on a flavor and have a tasting to make up their minds about how the cake is supposed to be. So they are working on that one right now. They have to travel to Memphis to do that. The cake doesn't sound serious at all, but it always gets to be an important thing. If it works, sometimes you can keep the top layer in the freezer for the wedding couple to have on their anniversary. I know in the case of our cake, we had some bad weather that knocked the freezer out, so the top of our cake was a big mush on our anniversary, unfortunately. There are all kinds of funny little things that go along with the wedding, and they have to be planned and traditions adhered to.

John and Sarah have already gone to choose the china pattern that they want. All these little things have been taken care of as we go along.

John came up yesterday afternoon and spent some time with me. He is so sweet about doing that. John and his sister Sallie and their mother Susan lived with me in Number 10 Middleton Park for about six or eight years or longer. That's the little boy that sat by me in church for a number of years. I used to help with him when he was at the age when children wiggle. (When he was very small, I once held him up so he could see something in church, and he grabbed hold of my earring. It didn't proceed to bleed until we left church, and then it did.)

I would not say he's more special than the other grandsons, and there are six, but I do have a special affection for him. I have been very close to him because of that physical proximity when he was growing up. Also, he and his friends had birthday parties at that house. So I wasn't as in tune to some of the other grandchildren's activities as I was with John's.

When John was here, he told me all about his new job and how excited he is about it and how much he loves the people he is working with. It's nice to see somebody as enthusiastic as he is. He is pretty levelheaded. He is just loaded with everything good that is going for him now. All in all, the world to him, aside from what we are seeing everywhere, looks pretty good. He doesn't mind letting people know that he's excited and that he is pleased about something. He makes no effort to be cool. So I like his attitude about things. He is fun to know.

That wedding is the big thing that I am looking forward to in the fall. Nearly everybody will be involved that can be. I think it is amazing to have as many nice things coming up as I have, and I appreciate so much being able to look forward to so many good things.

I skipped September. We have another baby coming in September. That's my daughter Sallie's daughter Sarah. She has this baby coming in mid-September, but we don't yet know if it's a boy or a girl. So I am on tenterhooks because I really like to have a name, if possible. Then I begin to list the whole family. Alexander already has his spot. I hope they don't change his name.

Since I began telling these stories, I have gone from last Thanksgiving, when all our family was gathered here for a great meal and a family photograph the next day, to planning the wedding on Thanksgiving weekend of my grandson John, which will be another gathering of the whole family to give thanks for and celebrate the beginning of a new branch of our family. This is truly a spectacular year.

When India was here, she learned to stand and walk by pulling up on my rolling walker. She learned to walk up here in my room. Not walk, run.

She had on little black shoes, and she flew everywhere. When she comes now, she knows where everything in this whole place is. She is very animated and awfully cute. There is a picture on Facebook of her being interviewed for nursery school. She sat by her father while she was being interviewed, straight as a stick, little feet sticking out in front and looking at people answering questions the best she can. She doesn't talk very well yet, which accounts for calling the new baby Zander. She will be going three days a week to playschool in Atlanta.

The youngest great-grandchild is Read and Danielle Talley's little girl. She was born in the fall, Reagan Hicks Talley. If Reagan sees something she likes, her face lights up. Sometimes when she sees me, she recognizes this walker better than she does me. It looks like it's her old friend. And I can see why. It's got wheels, handles to grip, and a compartment to put things in. It's a great little gym for a toddler. She is sweet and patient and full of smiles, but she's not on the hoof yet. She is sitting up very well now, but it won't be long before those feet start going. That's the fun of it. So when she gets going we'll know who she is. She is very even-tempered as far as I can tell, and I am looking forward to watching her personality come out as she grows older.

Of course I'm looking forward to meeting India's little brother and seeing what her reaction to a little brother is. She knows he is coming, and she already says "brother." Alexander is due very shortly now. I'm not answering the telephone real quick because it's too soon yet, but when we ease into May, I will be waiting for that call.

Oh Yes, My Birthday, and Other Journeys

Oh, I left something out when talking about May. I'll be 87 on May 19. The baby is supposed to come first. Nobody who is 87 should expect a summer to be lined up the way mine seems to be. I'm excited and very grateful.

My oldest daughter Judy is just back from taking her daughter Jennifer, her husband Matt, and their daughter Julia Claire to Italy. I had my fingers crossed the whole time. I've been to Italy with Judy twice. We had the most wonderful time. I have a book of pictures she had taken when we went together. On the day they were leaving, I looked at all her pictures and remembered all kinds of things. She wanted to share Italy with Julia Claire. We don't know how much longer it will be safe to go to Italy or anywhere else for that matter. We live in such a crazy world.

They had a wonderful time. They spent Palm Sunday in Rome and Easter in Venice. I can't think of two nicer places to be. Julia Claire is just short of ten, so she was looking forward to all the things her grandmother had told her to be watching for. They saw everything and Julia Claire loved everything. She liked Rome the very best. She's old enough to know a good deal of history.

I was sorry that they couldn't do quite as many things as Judy and I had done before. She saw some pictures Judy had taken before, and she said, "Emmie," which is what she calls her grandmother Judy, "I don't think that looks like a very good neighborhood." Actually the pictures were taken in a perfectly lovely neighborhood, but it didn't look like what she is familiar with. Julia Claire is making some notes on her thoughts from what she saw on her trip. I'm so glad that they got to go and that there was nothing scary about it. It all worked out.

Sallie, Susan's daughter, took a trip that scared me quite a bit earlier this year. I was so relieved when she came back home safely. She was in Hungary, parts of Germany, and Italy as well. I'm awfully glad that's over. I did hold my breath about that one. Too much was going on over there this year and none of it was very savory. I thought it was the sort of thing I didn't want her to get mixed up in. They got away with it. It was about six or eight months ago now. But I do want my grandchildren to know about the world as much as they can.

I think I want to hang on a long time and see what happens next. But I like my own world and am very grateful for it. When I compare it to the situations some of my contemporaries are in, and not too many are still around, I am humbled and grateful for the opportunity I have had to be here to see our family grow and branch out as it has. I have met so many nice people, and I'm so glad about the new ones coming to join us.

I watch my grandchildren grow and mature and become involved in their work and their own families; I love seeing them becoming who they are going to be. It doesn't bother me at all that they are no longer children, little like they used to be. I have a friend who cuts my hair every so often, and she has a grandson who is about eighteen now. She does nothing but complain, saying, "Oh, he's not the same sweet little boy he was. I loved him so when he was little."

He is doing some lovely things, and I keep saying, "Linda, please don't look at it that way. You would have prayed for him to do just what he is doing now, growing up and learning to drive. He comes back and keeps you in touch with what he is doing."

But she spends so much time saying, "Oh, it just makes me so sad; he's not the same little boy."

"Please don't do that to yourself," I say, "and don't do it to him."

We go in the same circles every time I have to go and get my hair cut. It just makes me sad, and it's not fair to the boy. Brooks is trying to be very devoted. But, "Oh, he's driving now."

Well, yes, but I say, "You'd feel bad if he couldn't drive. You'd feel bad if he had some major handicap that kept him from developing. You want him to grow and become who he is supposed to be. Don't be sad about it! Let him know how proud you are of him." I feel that way intensely about each one of my grandchildren. It's so exciting to see them, as adults, enjoy each other so much. There were times earlier this year that they were off in all directions, and I had concerns for them; but they're home now, and they learned from their trips. Now they are excited about what they are doing in the wide world.

We're from all over the place, and we have come together somehow in Nashville. I find it absolutely miraculous how people do encounter each other. My granddaughter Octavia, the aunt of the little boy we are expecting any minute, lives in New York City and has a great job that she enjoys thoroughly. She is a delight. Her father is David Obolensky—that's a Russian name, and quite an illustrious one, actually. I'm sure David was never expected to live in Nashville, Tennessee, because he grew up in several faraway places, and he was in Europe to some extent with his mother and father. When visiting a friend in Nashville, he went to Moon's Drugstore on Harding Road with another friend and met Cathy. The friend introduced them, and they started dating and eventually got married. That's just kind of miraculous. As the wedding was here, I met their family. Quite a few of them travelled all the way here from Europe. David has a sister who lives in Belgium. When I start to worry about her, I am told no one would tangle with her. Let's just say she has such a self-assured attitude that no one else worries about her, but I do.

A Story for the Grandchildren

In my dreams the other night I was remembering a story George used to tell about something that happened in the Philippines during the war. He would show a picture of the cathedral in Manilla that looked like it had been bombed out, though I don't know if it had been. Maybe it was just very old. He remembered going on hunting trips with one of the guys in the Navy. They had a little time off so they went hunting up in the mountains of Manila. There were pygmies that lived in the jungle. George and his friend had been warned about what to do and what to say if they met any pygmies in the jungle. They were well into the jungle once when all of a sudden they realized they were not alone. They were surrounded by pygmies with blowguns. They called them the Negritos. This sounds like a fairy tale, but it's absolutely true. I've seen some pictures of two or three of them.

It was scary, and he didn't know any of the language. He'd been told to ask to see the pygmy chief, but under the stress of the situation, he was having the hardest time remembering his name. It seems that those blowguns took up most of his brainpower. He finally pulled the name up in his memory and asked to see Manuel. They motioned for them to come on. About six pygmies led them through the jungle until they found themselves face to face with Manuel, the chief, who greeted them in a friendly way. They shook hands and were invited to stay, but they didn't linger long enough for dinner. George thought they would be better off that way. The pygmies had the reputation of being not too fastidious about what they ate.

George said they really did look the way you would think pygmies would look, with loincloths and blowguns and so forth. The whole year they were there in that area, they visited Manuel and his tribe several times and made friends. Manuel knew some English, so they were able to exchange a few very simple sentences. Think how funny it would have looked to see the man who wasn't four feet tall standing beside George, who was six feet four. George said, "I don't know why we were scared. We shouldn't have been." On the other hand, the pygmies proved to them that the darts they used for their blowguns really were poisonous.

That was a story that as the grandsons got older, George would have enjoyed telling them so much. I regret George was not able to tell them that story himself. He only knew John as a baby. McClain was a little bit older, and he knew Jason and Read. Of course, he never knew his grandson Thomas. The girls are a bit older, so he knew Jennifer, and Cathy's two girls, and Sarah. But most of them were quite young when he died, and some he never knew. I find that extremely sad because knowing them would have enriched his life—and theirs—considerably. He would have loved telling them about his Navy experience and the friends he made in different parts of the world.

Flan in my Dreams

The idea to include the following story came to me in a dream. I realized in my subconscious that I would not want to leave this out.

I had a dream about Cleo the other day. She makes a really good flan, which is a kind of custard; and the other day she had made one, but I went to bed without eating any of it because it had not yet set up. Very late that same night, I saw Cleo standing by the bed with a piece of flan on the little tray that she puts it on, and she said, "I know this is late, but here it is if you'd like." She had her hat on, as if she were going to church. I was thinking about it and thinking about it and then said, "What time is it?" I got out of bed. It was 2:30 a.m. I went all the way around my room and looked on my chest to be sure it wasn't there, because if it was, I would have eaten it, even at 2:30. Maybe especially at 2:30! It might have been better. She makes such a good one, and it sets up so well.

I asked her the next morning, "Did you come in here at 2:30? I looked for the flan, but couldn't find it."

She said, "I wasn't here at 2:30!" But the dream seemed so real. I told her what she had had on and everything. So I seem to dream a little. My dreams seem to be coming back and forth a little strangely. Normally I don't dream at all, or almost never.

Hopes and Dreams for the Cousins

I hope the little ones that are coming along now love their cousins as much as our now grown-up cousins do. They meet at each other's houses and they somehow keep up. That's one good thing about these telephones. They make it easy for cousins to check on each other. Every now and again somebody comes and tells me something I didn't know, which I really love. Sarah Stringfellow, the girl that John's marrying, brought me some sketches of the bridesmaid dresses. That's really sweet for an old grandmother, you know. They have honored me by keeping me informed about wedding cakes, wedding dresses, china patterns, and all the little things that go along with weddings. I guess they know how much I care about that kind of thing. I love the way they include me in this part of their lives.

Somehow they seem to grasp that I care, in a big way. I'm butting into all kinds of things all the time. Like what? Well, I've seen the church where the wedding is going to be when I was in Memphis. I don't go to Memphis very often, but I've seen the church because John and Sarah were so anxious that I get there and see it. It's about 150 years old, St. Mary's Church, a Catholic church in downtown Memphis. It's got more statues than I've seen in a church in years. Just going into the church is like walking into another world in many ways. There are big ceilings and a wide center aisle, thank goodness. I don't know how to function very well in churches that have two aisles with all the seating in the middle. That doesn't feel like a church to me. I don't understand churches like that at all. It's a little Baptist, which is fine, but that's not how I understand a church. Churches like that seem more like auditoriums than churches. The architecture is like that out at St. Henry's, which has three aisles somehow.

The baptismal font is close to the front door as you go in, and that's where it ought to be. The floors creak a little, and it smells right. John and Sarah went for the first time to look at it as a service was ending. They stood in the back until it was over. People were coming out, and whoever was showing them around the church explained to some of the people leaving that they were a young couple who would be married there in the fall. They said, "Oh, tell us all about it!" John and Sarah were completely surrounded by parishioners who wanted to know everything. John ended up giving them the date saying, "We hope you'll all come." They probably will. Sarah said they were so enthusiastic and wanted to be there, and were so glad to know it was not going to be a night-time wedding because those are awkward for them, as many of them are quite elderly.

Sarah grew up in Memphis. After the wedding, they will live here in Nashville. John has a little house they are going to fix up before the wedding. The parish church Sarah grew up in is further out, and they thought that, for out-of-town guests, it would be an awkward place to have the wedding. I think her own priest suggested that they use St. Mary's because it would be closer to the hotels and the rehearsal dinner. So that's how this church was chosen. John and Sarah are so excited about this church. That's my little John.

I think it's interesting that John chose to bring a new Sarah into the family. There are already so many! Our family produces and draws to it Sarahs and Sallies quite prolifically. These names have been carried on in our family for several generations.

Stories of Sarahs

There is an interesting story about a Sarah that involved my mother and my grandmother. My grandmother got a note from school saying, "Your daughter is impudent." Grandmother went steaming in to talk to the teacher.

She said, "I can't imagine how my daughter could have been impudent. That's not this child."

The teacher said, "Well, she doesn't answer to her name."

Grandmother suspected what was wrong. She asked, "What are you calling her?"

The teacher said, "I call her by her proper name, Sarah."

My grandmother said, "She doesn't answer to 'Sarah.' Her grandmother and her great grandmother are 'Sallie.' Of course she doesn't answer to 'Sarah.' She has an Aunt Sarah, but that's not her name and of course she doesn't answer to it."

The teacher had assumed that 'Sallie' was always a nickname for 'Sarah.' I will say I think Grandmother got that straightened out.

The Sallie with *ie* was my grandfather's mother. She was Miss Sallie Bush and she married Thomas L. Herbert. The name Sallie came on down. There are also a few Sarahs. My grandfather had a sister named Sarah whom we called Aunt Sarah, and there was no confusion between Aunt Sarah and the Sallies in the family. I've probably held on to that name longer than anybody else in that generation. It is funny how often *Sarah* and *Sallie* pop up among friends and, of course, new relatives. *Sarah Stringfellow*, I love *Stringfellow*; I think it's a wonderful name. She really is a Sarah, and she is interesting because on the Stringfellow side her grandparents are very English. I don't remember what the other grandparents are called—I swear my mind is going—but their name is Spanish. Sarah looks a little Spanish with long, dark hair. I have met both sets of grandparents, and they are charming. Susan had a luncheon for them here at her house. Sarah's father Alec is very tall and just as nice as he can be. In some way he is involved with literary work. When John went to ask him for her hand in marriage he wasn't too nervous about it, because he has visited them in Memphis a number of times. What Alec said was, "What took you so long?"

Sarah's mother Maria is a teacher. She is a lovely person. The fact that there is Latin blood in her family makes them particularly interesting. Sarah has two brothers, Alexander and Samuel. They both have married within the last couple of years. One is already a father and the other soon will be. Both families seem to be blooming. They were all here for the lunch. Susan went to some trouble to get a very nice lunch together. John had been invited to the brothers' weddings as Sarah's beau. They all get along so well. Sallie, my granddaughter, will be a bridesmaid in John and Sarah's wedding, along with Sarah's friends. John has a gaggle of friends who are going down to support him in November. It's going to be a festival.

April 11, 2016

EPILOGUE
To My Children:

Judy, Cathy, Sallie, George, Susan, & Robin

As I look back and remember our lives together, I know each one of you will have a somewhat different memory of what happened. I will have forgotten a great deal. (I hope I don't make up things that didn't happen, but that's the way I tend to remember things!) The memories and stories all come rapidly, at different times, and my enjoyment in reliving our joint lives is overwhelming because I have so much to remember. I am sure I don't remember it all exactly right. Each of you could correct and adjust my stories, but I do this with enormous pleasure because you've all contributed enormously to me and to my life. I'm happy and overjoyed with the pleasure of these great memories that each one of you has given me. I hope these remembrances, many of which you asked me about and brought to mind, bring you a lot of pleasure, too. I'm sure these recollections are not orderly. This is likely not to be the way you will remember what happened, but I ask you to trust that I got one main thing right about our lives.

One thing I know is that a great deal of laughter goes through our interwoven stories, even the memories of mishaps and hospital visits, along with events that, at the time, we thought were disasters. I think that every one of the children has the ability, which you get from your father, to see the absurdity of things. As we go forward, this ability helps us keep balanced, I hope. I am very grateful for the sense of humor that all of us seem to have. I think it's a great gift. You have all been a great gift to me, every last one of you. Now I am looking forward to the great-grandchildren and all the special occasions in their future. Some of what I am looking forward to I may not see. Smile and laugh through these events. You might think, "Mama would have liked this," but enjoy it yourself.

I would hope you will be able to find love and beauty around you and in each other all your lives. Always look for something that makes you smile out of what happens, because things can seem pretty drab and catastrophic, but they're not. Whatever happens, there will be a place for it, and it will fit in the scheme of your lives and what you do.

When you were children, and you would leave our home, and I would watch you going down the driveway, the last thing I remember always saying to you is this: "Take good care of each other." I will still keep saying that. You're long and tall and have families of your own, and your own families, jobs, and activities are all terribly important, but I still say, "Take good care of each other." Do that, and I am convinced it will bring you happiness.

You've certainly brought me nothing but happiness. We've shed a tear or two here and there, for one reason or another, but the life I am looking back at has been a blessing all the way through. Each one of you has given me so much pleasure, and I trust my pride in you as my family is forgivable. As you find a little time in your lives, think back to the grandparents and great-grandparents that you know about, and the family that you are continuing, because you are all part of a chain. All of us are. It's a great privilege to know each one of you. I won't be able to go all the way with you, but bear in mind that I hope you find continual happiness in every day you live. I love you all.

I have wanted everyone to find the humor in life and to be happy in every day of life ever since Judy was old enough to drive. She got her driver's license when she was fifteen because I couldn't drive her or the children anywhere, and she was conscientious about all things. She would drive to school, to the grocery store, and to church. She was so responsible and so wonderful about doing this for our family ever since she drove a back seat full of little children to kindergarten at Overbrook. At times you probably wanted to clap your hands over your ears, because I said it so much. "Take good care of each other." And you have.

April 16, 2016

AFTERWORD

Down Open Roads

When my old friend and fourth-through-twelfth-grade classmate, George Hicks, called from Nashville in October of 2015, it was early on a bright California morning. My wife and I had come to Los Angeles to visit our son during Family Weekend at college, and I was sitting down to work a couple of hours before we would go see him on campus. Much to my delight, George wanted me to help his mother tell her life story, and to get started as soon as I could. He had learned that I was working as a personal historian, helping people collect their family stories and write their memoirs. From the very start, he believed his mother would take to a structured way of gathering her memories and telling her stories. Sallie Hicks' mobility had recently become more limited than it had been, so she wasn't able to be as active as her lively mind, generous spirit, and creative imagination inspired her to be. George knew everyone in his family would love to have her stories in book form. When we were through talking, Sallie and I had a new project to work on.

We began on the first Monday in November 2015. I went to her home in Middleton Park, which she shares with the family of her daughter Susan, and climbed the stairs to the floor she now inhabits with her dog Murphy. As soon as she saw me, she overflowed with the joy, graciousness, and self-deprecating humility that mysteriously co-exist with tremendous energy and unflagging will in her petite, still girlish form. In the course of our interviews, on more than one occasion after an hour and a half of non-stop tale-telling, I would say, "This seems like a good place to stop for now," only to have her plough forward with more stories demanding to be heard immediately, lest they slip from present memory. I settled back into my chair and tried not to interfere, occasionally checking my digital recorder to make sure it had not drowned in the cascade of words. The stories just kept coming, as anyone who reads this book can see.

She began our first interview looking forward to gathering the whole family for Thanksgiving, a total of thirty-two children, grandchildren, spouses, and great-grandchildren. A photograph taken the next day proves the reality of what Sallie celebrates so richly in her recollections of that day. She concluded our final interview in April 2016 by looking forward to the year ahead, which would culminate on the Saturday after Thanksgiving 2016. On that day, almost everyone in the family would reassemble in Memphis for the wedding of her grandson John Thetford and his fiancée Sarah Stringfellow, the latest new family to branch out from the family Sallie and George began on their *weddings* day almost seventy years before. From one Thanksgiving to another, Sallie's happy perspective on life and family has shaped these memories into what is truly "A Year of Thanksgivings."

As I got acquainted with Sallie, I became infected by her enthusiasm for the beauty and humor she has found in the world all her life. I shared her appreciation for a bouquet of peonies, even though an unseen bee would sting her. I felt her excitement at the spectacle of Broadway's *Babes in Toyland*, though it was the need for an eye surgery that caused her to travel to New York City where the musical was performed. I was moved by her delight in the antique chandelier her mother found on Royal Street in New Orleans days after Sallie's high-school graduation ceremony, though her diploma bore no signature but her own tears. Here was a lady who did not waste time or energy fretting over what she could not do. At an early age, with the help of those who loved her, she began to make her own best life, as she put it, by going "down the roads that were open to me."

While going down those roads, she won the heart of the man who was to be her husband and the father of the grand family they would have, George Thomas Hicks. It was love for Sallie that taught this young man full of his own thoughts, experiences, and abilities to put his arm out whenever they walked together where she might miss a step, and Sallie never forgot. He filled her thoughts on Thanksgiving Day 2015 as all their descendants gathered on her front porch steps for one of those historic, once-in-a-lifetime photographs. She shares with us the joyful ecstasy she feels in the family God has created and continues to bring forth from the fruit of her marriage to George.

Early in our interviews, I knew her memories would take me, and ultimately her readers, through a new world of many joys happily shared and a few sorrows endured without complaint. Tales of ecstatic children celebrating tadpoles becoming frogs blend with the hinted consolation found in years of attendance at daily Mass after the premature death of her husband to make a rich and varied gift of life, a life blessed by the heart of one grateful lady who could not love her family more.

When we were finished with our interviews, I would call to ask her a question about some detail that needed clarification, and she would tell me things I just couldn't let slip away, in spite of the fact that we had more than enough to work with already. Once she asked if she told me about the times

George would wake her up in the middle of the night and tell her, "Let's go out and walk in the moonlight!" She would put on her bathrobe and boots, take the outreached hand of her husband, and join him for a midnight stroll in the silver, dewy pasture; and they would revel in the beauty unseen by everyone else but the eye of God.

She still has more than enough enthusiasm for one person, so she shares it freely with anyone who will listen. I think she only gave one reflection on growing old, perhaps because she hardly thinks of herself as being old at all. Her words explain why. "I grew up with grandmothers who almost got to be a hundred years old, so I have been around old people since I was very young. I used to think that when you got to be as old as I am now, there was nothing left. I was so wrong! When you keep making new discoveries at eighty-seven, life is pretty wonderful."

Sallie continues to be one of the most grateful people I have ever known. May her spirit of gratitude fill your heart and mind so that, by knowing Sallie a little better through the stories told in these pages, you may have "a year of thanksgivings" every year.

Joseph N. Davis

July 28, 2016

TIMELINE

4/17/1904	Robert Read, Sallie's father, is born.
8/12/1910	Sallie Herbert, Sallie's mother, is born.
5/7/1924	George Thomas Hicks is born.
5/19/1929	Sallie Read is born in Nashville, TN.
1932	Sallie's family moves to Pewee Valley.
5/19/1938	Sallie is confirmed at St. James' Episcopal Church, Pewee Valley.
Fall 1938	Sallie enters fourth grade at Louisville Collegiate School.
1941	Sallie's father accepts post as assistant treasurer with Alcoa in Pittsburgh, where Sallie skips seventh grade and enters eighth grade at Winchester Thurston School. Julia Herbert takes Sallie to Marian Anderson concert.
Fall 1942	Sallie moves to Nashville and attends Ward Belmont as a boarding student.
Early 1946	George is discharged from the Navy. Sallie and George go on a blind date.
Spring 1946	Sallie completes her high-school education.
Fall 1946	George and Sallie go to a Vanderbilt football game.
4/20/1950	Sallie and George are married and move into a house on Belle Meade Blvd. that George built.
1/28/1951	Julia Ann Hicks (Judy) is born.
10/7/1952	Mary Catharine Hicks (Catharine) is born.
1953	Family moves to Louisville.

1954	Sallie joins the Roman Catholic Church.
1955	Family moves back to Nashville and lives on River Road.
9/26/1955	Sallie Read Hicks (Sallie) is born.
1956	The family moves to home that George built at 2228 Old Hickory Blvd., which is later called "Knollwood Stables."
9/6/1957	George Thomas Hicks, Jr., is born.
2/1960	Death of Sallie's Grandfather Read.
4/22/1960	Susan Herbert Hicks (Susan) is born.
7/27/1961	Robin Withers Hicks (Robin) is born.
ca. 1961	George brings home a trailer full of ponies.
1968	Grandmother Hicks (referred to as "Mom" by the family) moves in.
3/3/1973	Grandmother Hicks dies.
1984	Sallie's husband, George, has an aortal dissection.
4/20/1989	Death of Sallie's father, Robert Read.
1989-1991	George builds the 10 Middleton Park Lane house.
1991	Sallie and George move into the home at 10 Middleton Park Lane, Nashville.
1991	Sallie Read moves into the home at 10 Middleton Park Lane, Nashville.
5/27/1992	George, Sallie's husband, dies in Switzerland.
8/4/97	Death of Sallie Read.
2008	Sallie and Susan design and build their current home and move into it with Susan's children.
11/28/15	Family portrait is taken on front porch of Sallie's home.
11/26/16	Wedding of John Thetford and Sarah Stringfellow.

IMMEDIATE ANCESTORS OF SALLIE READ HICKS

Col. Robert Enoch Withers (1821 - 1907) m. Mary V. Royall

11 daughters and 1 son

Josephine Withers (1854 - 1956) m. Dr. John Read (1849-1892)

2 sons

Robert E. Read (1878 - 1960) m. Sue Rector (1880 - ?)

Robert Rector Read (1904 - 1989), Sallie Read Hicks' father

Josephine Withers Read (1906 - ?)

Robert N. Herbert (1811 - 1888) m. Elizabeth L. Cummins (1814 - 1895)

Thomas Levins Herbert (1852 - 1913) m. Sallie Bush (1854 - 1917)

Thomas Levins Herbert, Jr. (1883 - 1959) m. Julia Ann Robards (1883 - 1973)

T L Herbert, III (1908 – 1909)

Sallie Herbert (1910 - 1997), Sallie Read Hicks' mother

* * * * *

Robert Rector Read (1904 - 1989) m. Sallie Herbert (1910 - 1997)

Sallie Read (1929)

IMMEDIATE ANCESTORS OF GEORGE THOMAS HICKS

George Washington Hicks (1835 - 1898) m. Mary Ann Cayce (1839 - 1873)

George Washington Hicks (1867 - 1918) m. Mary Watson (1863 - 1934)

George Lemuel Hicks (1889 - 1937), George Thomas Hicks' father

Frank Schweinhart (1823 – 1880) m. Elizabeth Schweinhart (1820 – 1895)

(They emigrated from Germany to Louisville, KY.)

Charles Eberenz (1859 - 1921) m. Cecilia Schweinhart (? - 1917)

Nine children (Catharine was number 4.)

Catharine Eberenz (1890 - 1973), George Thomas Hicks' mother

Charles Eberenz m. Carrie Dimner (1863 - 1921)

* * * * *

George Lemuel Hicks (1889 - 1937) m. Catharine Eberenz (1890 - 1973)

Charles Burton Hicks (1911 - 1996)

Mary Hicks Proctor (1912 - 2001)

George Thomas Hicks (5/7/24 - 5/27/92)

FAMILY TREE

George & Sallie Hicks
m. April 20, 1950

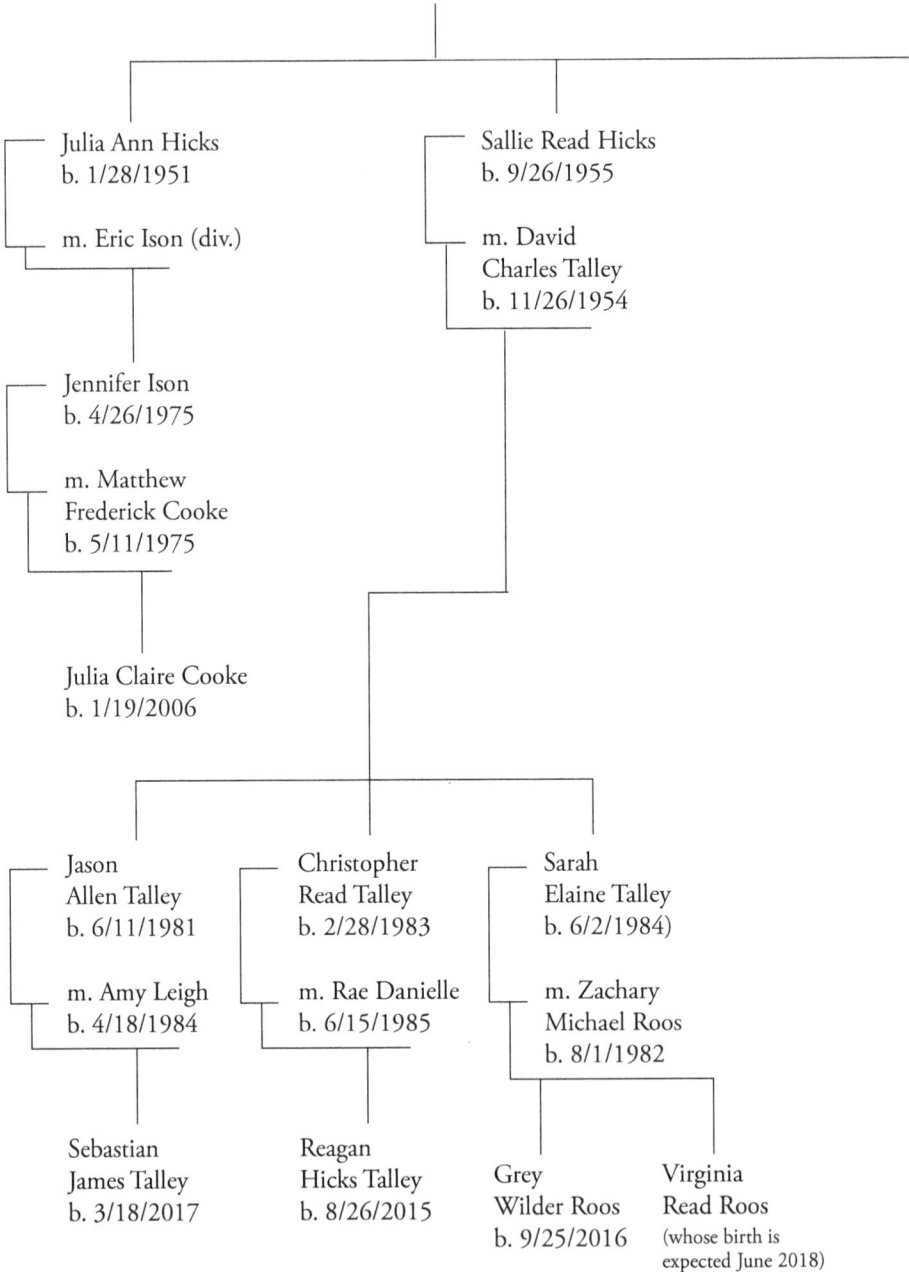

Julia Ann Hicks
b. 1/28/1951

m. Eric Ison (div.)

Jennifer Ison
b. 4/26/1975

m. Matthew
Frederick Cooke
b. 5/11/1975

Julia Claire Cooke
b. 1/19/2006

Sallie Read Hicks
b. 9/26/1955

m. David
Charles Talley
b. 11/26/1954

Jason
Allen Talley
b. 6/11/1981

m. Amy Leigh
b. 4/18/1984

Sebastian
James Talley
b. 3/18/2017

Christopher
Read Talley
b. 2/28/1983

m. Rae Danielle
b. 6/15/1985

Reagan
Hicks Talley
b. 8/26/2015

Sarah
Elaine Talley
b. 6/2/1984)

m. Zachary
Michael Roos
b. 8/1/1982

Grey
Wilder Roos
b. 9/25/2016

Virginia
Read Roos
(whose birth is
expected June 2018)

(figure 1.)

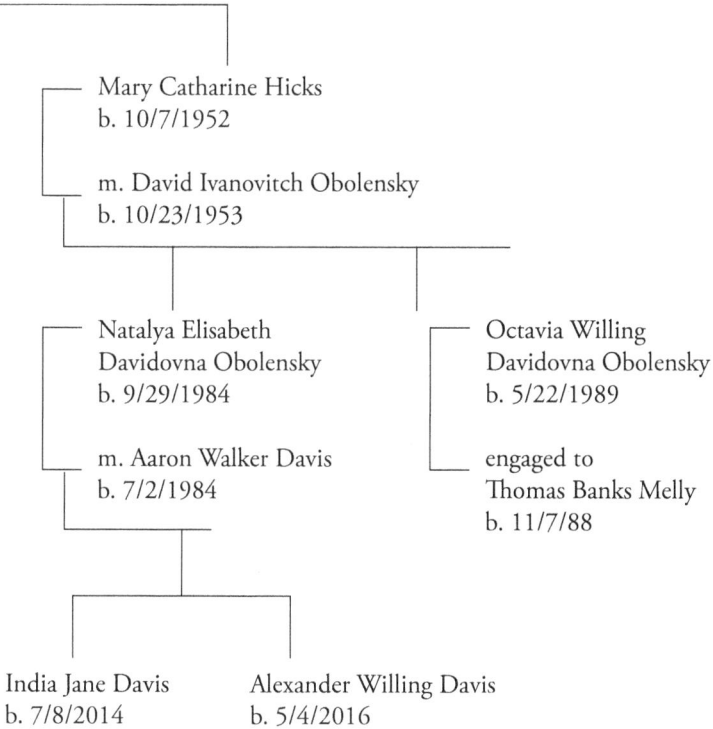

Mary Catharine Hicks
b. 10/7/1952

m. David Ivanovitch Obolensky
b. 10/23/1953

Natalya Elisabeth
Davidovna Obolensky
b. 9/29/1984

m. Aaron Walker Davis
b. 7/2/1984

Octavia Willing
Davidovna Obolensky
b. 5/22/1989

engaged to
Thomas Banks Melly
b. 11/7/88

India Jane Davis
b. 7/8/2014

Alexander Willing Davis
b. 5/4/2016

FAMILY TREE

(continued)

George & Sallie Hicks
m. April 20, 1950

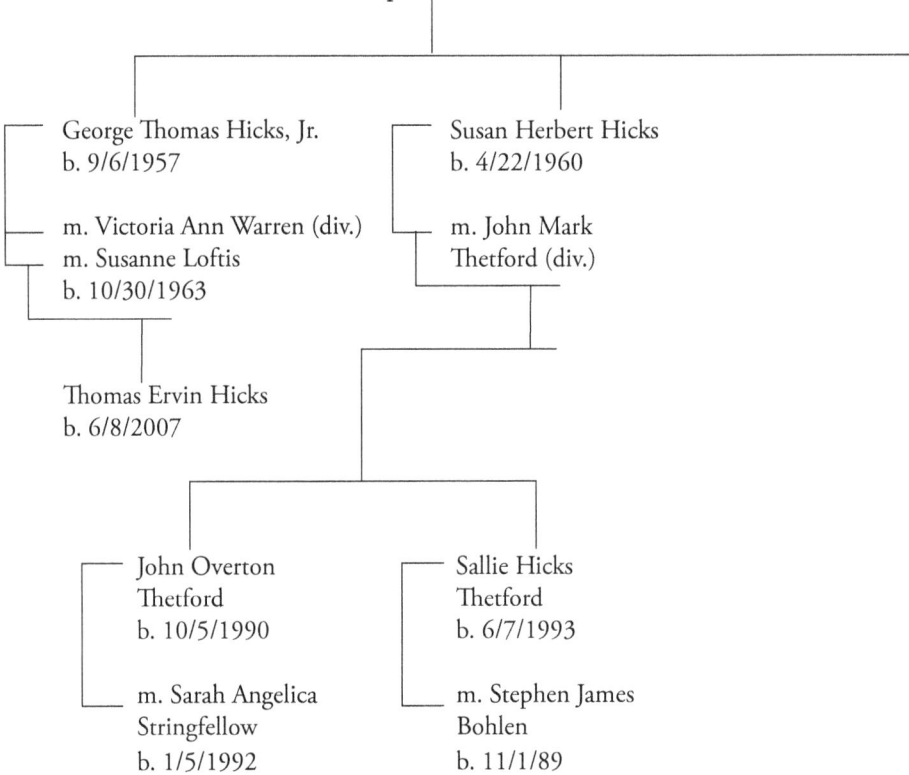

- George Thomas Hicks, Jr.
  b. 9/6/1957

  m. Victoria Ann Warren (div.)
  m. Susanne Loftis
  b. 10/30/1963
  - Thomas Ervin Hicks
    b. 6/8/2007
- Susan Herbert Hicks
  b. 4/22/1960

  m. John Mark
  Thetford (div.)
  - John Overton
    Thetford
    b. 10/5/1990

    m. Sarah Angelica
    Stringfellow
    b. 1/5/1992
  - Sallie Hicks
    Thetford
    b. 6/7/1993

    m. Stephen James
    Bohlen
    b. 11/1/89

(figure 2.)

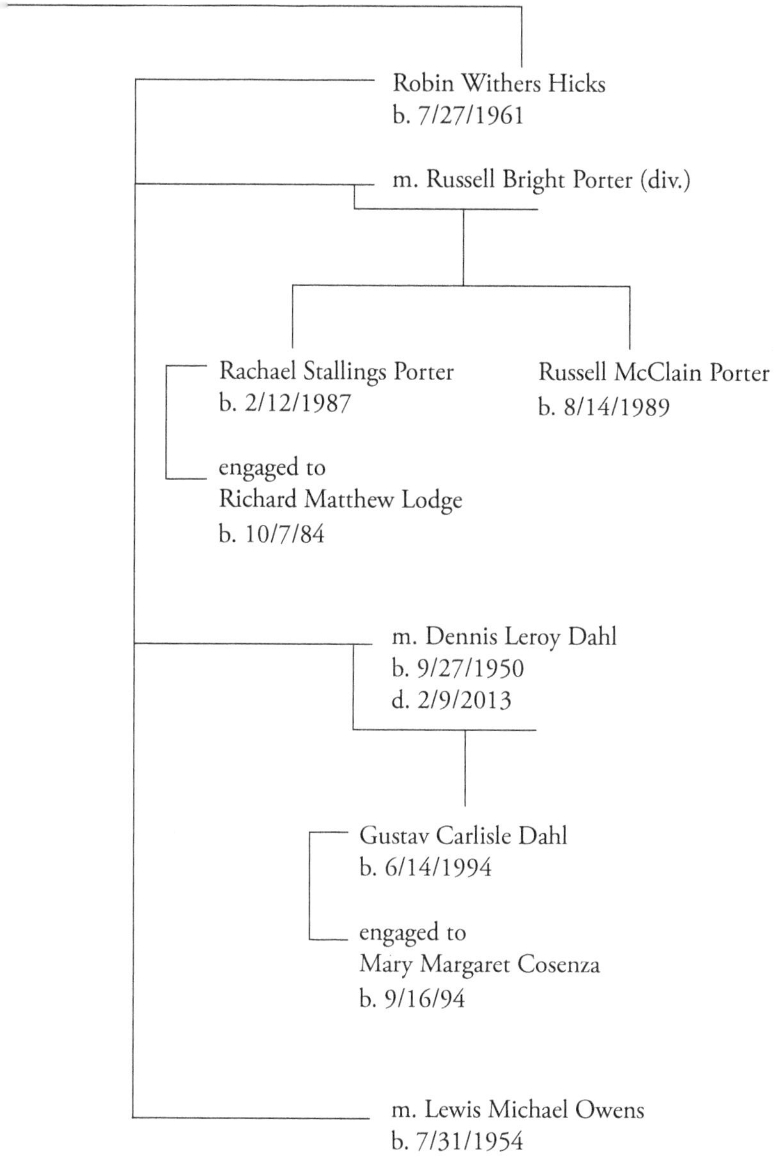
Robin Withers Hicks
b. 7/27/1961
m. Russell Bright Porter (div.)
Rachael Stallings Porter
b. 2/12/1987
engaged to
Richard Matthew Lodge
b. 10/7/84
Russell McClain Porter
b. 8/14/1989
m. Dennis Leroy Dahl
b. 9/27/1950
d. 2/9/2013
Gustav Carlisle Dahl
b. 6/14/1994
engaged to
Mary Margaret Cosenza
b. 9/16/94
m. Lewis Michael Owens
b. 7/31/1954

FAMILY PHOTOS

Sallie with Mary.

Sallie in her Collegiate uniform at the age of eight, midway through third grade, her first year there.

Sallie at a high school fraternity formal, before she had met George.

Sallie's mother, or "Big Sallie," as George called her.

Sallie with her grandparents Julia and TL Herbert and her parents Big Sallie and Robert Read at a pre-debutante occasion at the Belle Meade Country Club.

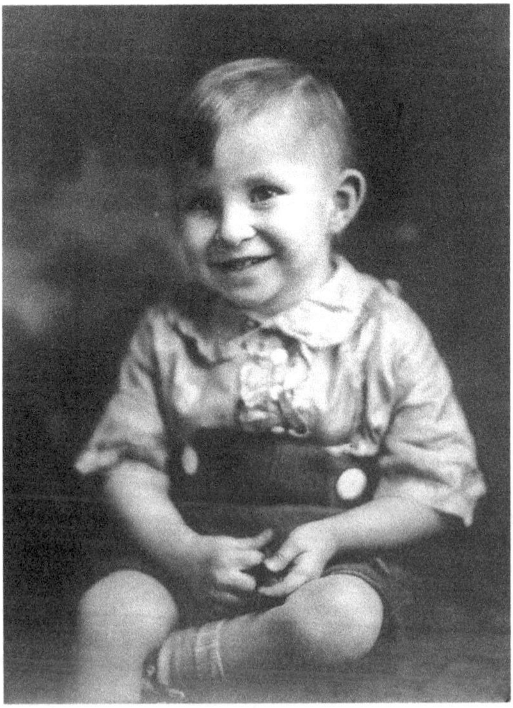

George as a two-year-old.

George as a two-year-old, his older siblings, Charles and Mary, and their parents, George L. and Catharine E. Hicks.

“Big George,” as he later became known,
in the in the V-12 program at Georgia Tech.

George at Georgia Tech having a picnic with Sue, who has been cut out by none other than Sallie herself.

The young couple at a party at the Bachelor's Club, which was always "tails."

Wedding picture taken in advance for the paper, at Grace's Shop for Ladies.

Wedding day, heading to Atlanta for wedding number two. Next stop, Casablanca.

Little Sallie, Sallie, Cathy and Judy, on the porch at St. George's Episcopal Church, before attending a wedding.

Portrait of the children taken in the basement of Rich Schwarz, at Belle Meade Plaza. Sallie is holding Evil, the cat. The portrait was Big Sallie's idea, so that George would have it during an upcoming two-week Naval Reserve trip. None of the children were happy about wearing the make-up required by the photographer.

Little George, Little Sallie, Cathy, and Judy on our car trip to Mexico City by way of California and Guadalajara in a station wagon named Armageddon, our beat-up Oldsmobile with a backward-facing back seat. The next year, it went to Expo '67 in Montreal.

Judy, Little Sallie, Robin, Susan, and Cathy all mounted up, riding Dixie Devil, Tear, Little Bit, Surprise, and Rambling Rose.

Sallie Herbert did a sketch of her father, TL Herbert, at Christmas. He's sitting in a little French Louis XVI chair, and he's gone to sleep. Her drawing looks just like him.

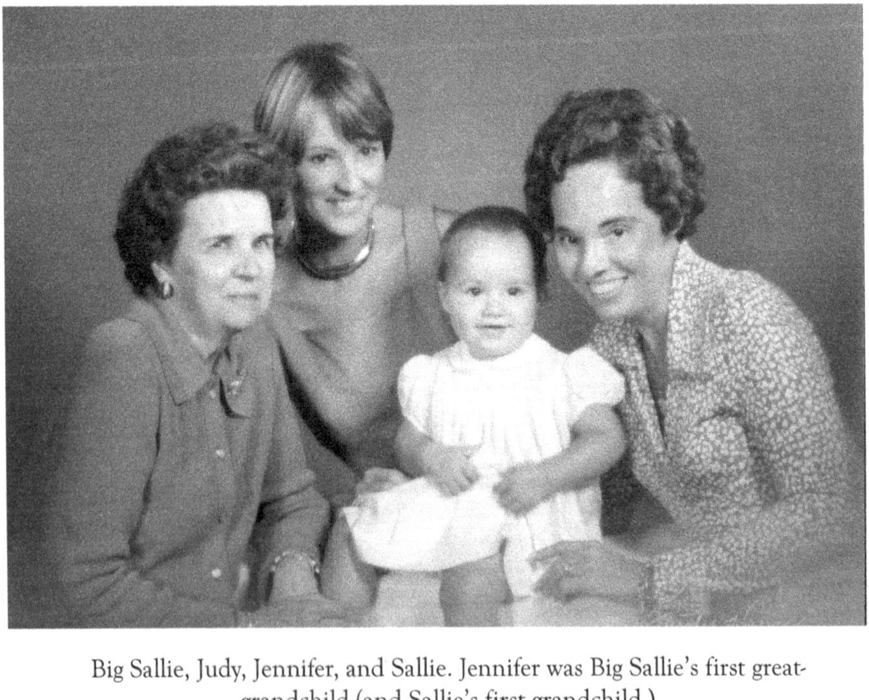

Big Sallie, Judy, Jennifer, and Sallie. Jennifer was Big Sallie's first great-grandchild (and Sallie's first grandchild.)

The home George and Charlie Warterfield designed and built at Middleton.

No caption needed. Taken at Robin's wedding.

Cathy, Susan, George, Sallie, Robin, Judy,
and the beaming Matriarch, November 27, 2015.

The twelve grandchildren and two great-grandchildren, November 27, 2015.

Wedding picture of John Thetford and Sarah Stringfellow, married in Memphis on November 26, 2016.

The whole extended clan, November 27, 2015.

Back Row: 1. David Obolensky 2. Cathy Obolensky 3. Octavia Obolensky 4. Sallie Talley 5. Danielle Talley 6. Reagan Talley 7. Read Talley 8. Jason Talley 9. Amy Talley 10. George Hicks 11. Sarah Talley Roos 12. Robin Dahl Owens 13. Suzanne Hicks, mostly hidden behind Susan Thetford 14. McClain Porter 15. Susan Thetford 16. Zach Roos 17. Rachael Porter 18. John Thetford 19. Matt Cooke. **Seated, Middle Row:** 20. John Mark Thetford 21. David Talley 22. Sallie Thetford Bohlen 23. Sallie Read Hicks 24. Jennifer Cooke 25. Judy Ison. **Seated, Front Row:** 26. Gus Dahl 27. Natalya Obolensky Davis 28. Aaron Davis 29. India Davis 30. Julia Clair Cooke 31. Thomas Hicks.
Not Pictured: Alexander Willing Davis, born 5/4/16; Gray Wilder Roos, born 9/25/2017; and Sebastian Talley, born in the spring of 2017.
Photo by Robert Michael Schiel, friend of Judy Ison

ABOUT THE AUTHORS

Because of a congenital eye condition, **Sallie Hicks** learned at an early age that she could not do many of the things girls her age took for granted, like team sports and seeing the blackboard in a classroom. Instead, she decided at an early age to "go down roads that were open to her." Enabled by remarkable storytelling gifts, for decades she has kept alive the memory of her forebears, and she has preserved the family stories that she helped create as the wife of prominent real estate developer and homebuilder George T. Hicks and mother of five daughters and one son. When asked to describe her life's work, she says that being a wife and mother to her family was "the point of the whole thing." Now in this book made from a series of interviews, she passes on a treasury of family stories and, along with it, her unforgettable personality and inspiring attitude towards life.

Sallie lives in Nashville, Tennessee, with her dog Murphy in a home she shares with her daughter Susan. From the sitting area of her bedroom, she rejoices in the steady flow of new stories about her growing number of great-grandchildren.

Joseph N. Davis grew up listening to memories recounted by elderly family storytellers from Tennessee and Mississippi while those around him said, "Somebody should write these stories down!" After organizing and editing his father's memoirs, he launched Talking Tree Tales in 2015 and began helping other people tell their stories. A graduate of the University of the

South, Joseph taught English before attending Nashotah House Theological Seminary and being ordained to the Episcopal priesthood. He currently serves as vicar of Grace Episcopal Church in Spring Hill, Tennessee. Reading, playing tennis, and early American music are among his favorite activities. He and his wife Cindy have two grown sons and live in Nashville with their dog Bo.

As a friend of Sallie's son George since fourth grade, Joseph considers it an honor to have worked with Sallie Hicks to preserve her memories and reflections. *A Year of Thanksgivings* is his first published book.

www.ingramcontent.com/pod-product-compliance
Lightning Source LLC
Chambersburg PA
CBHW031937090426
42811CB00002B/212
9780692976210